D1123763

Sermons in Stories
for Children

Sermons
in Stories
for Children

GRAHAM R. HODGES

ABINGDON PRESS
NEW YORK • NASHVILLE

SERMONS IN STORIES FOR CHILDREN

Copyright © MCMLIX by Abingdon Press

All rights in this book are reserved.
No part of the book may be reproduced in any
manner whatsoever without written permission of
the publishers except brief quotations embodied in
critical articles or reviews. For information address
Abingdon Press, Nashville 2, Tennessee.

Library of Congress Catalog Card Number: 59-10360

Scripture quotations unless otherwise noted are
from the Revised Standard Version of the Bible
and are copyright 1946 and 1952 by the Division
of Christian Education of the National Council of
the Churches of Christ in the U.S.A.

SET UP, PRINTED, AND BOUND BY THE
PARTHENON PRESS, AT NASHVILLE,
TENNESSEE, UNITED STATES OF AMERICA

Dedicated to
My loyal and good friends
In Ticonderoga and Crown Point, New York,
who were so kind to me and my family

PREFACE

ALL nature, the whole world, the mighty cosmos, and the tiniest bit of life about us literally cry out with a message of God's power, creativity, love, and care. We see him everywhere if we but stop to look and listen. Had we adults but the open mind of a child, our lives would be a ceaseless stretch of adoration.

These talks have been used in the Congregational churches of Ticonderoga, Crown Point, and Watertown, New York, to open the eyes of boys and girls to their heavenly Father. It is hoped that they also helped the adults listening in. Some are obviously too old for primary children.

To Mrs. Richard P. Downs of Ticonderoga I owe the ideas for the talks "The Magic Mirror" and "What Can I Do for You?" To the boys and girls who originally listened to all of these "children's sermons" with such attention, I give my thanks.

GRAHAM R. HODGES

CONTENTS

1. Who Rang the Bell for Dick Whittington?

"So then, as we have opportunity, let us do good to all men."—Gal. 6:10

DO YOU KNOW THE STORY OF DICK WHITTINGTON, THREE TIMES Lord Mayor of London, who died about the year 1423? He died extremely wealthy, having been in charge of the finances for the building of Westminster Abbey, and left his large fortune to many charitable organizations.

Three times he served his city as one of its greatest mayors. Although he was born the son of a knight and was well to do from the start, a curious legend later grew around his name which is even more interesting than the real story of this man, for it has fascinated people more than the true facts.

According to this legend, first put into writing in a play nearly two hundred years after Whittington's death, he was a poor orphan boy who made his living by washing pots and pans in a rich man's kitchen.

So discouraged was he that he started to flee from London and seek his fortune elsewhere. On the edge of the city he heard church bells ringing. He stopped to listen. Somehow they seemed to call his name. He listened further. They seemed to say something to him. What were the words he thought they said? "Turn again, Whittington, thrice Lord Mayor of London town." Again and again they repeated the message.

"Well," said the discouraged boy, "if that's true, then I'll return to my old home and job."

Just how he became rich and famous because of a cat is a story I want you to read for yourself.

What I want to know is this: Who rang the bell for Dick Whittington?

Certainly this unknown bell ringer had no idea he was reversing a lonely boy's whole destiny. How would he know who heard or cared for his ringing? Perhaps that day he didn't feel good and didn't want to ring the bells at all, but wanted to stay at home in bed. Or perhaps he didn't care to ring them well, as everybody took the bells for granted. He must have rung them with a certain rhythm to give Dick Whittington the message I've quoted.

Whoever it was, he rang the bells well and at the right time!

In a way we are all bell ringers like that unknown man or boy of the Dick Whittington legend. The way we live, the words we say, the books we read, the movies and TV programs we watch, our habits, our attendance or neglect of church and Sunday school, even the way we talk, smile, and walk, give a mysterious message to the whole world.

How do we know who's watching or listening, hoping to get some message of encouragement from us? No matter how weak or inferior or down the ladder we regard ourselves, somebody looks to us for example and guidance. We can make others sad, happy, blue, cheerful, good, bad, better, worse, or indifferent according to the way we conduct ourselves.

The Bible and many of our history books are full of unknown people whose examples make us better people today. Who were the brave soldiers who dared death from the Philistines to get their commander, David, a drink of water from the well at Bethlehem? What was the name of the slave maiden of Naaman, the mighty Syrian general's wife's servant, who gave her mistress instructions that cured Naaman of the disease of leprosy? We don't know.

What lad provided the five loaves and two fishes with which Jesus fed the multitude? What was the true name of the thief on the cross who repented in his last hours and went with our Lord to paradise? We don't know.

You, too, know people you admire, respect, and imitate. The chances are they are unaware of your feelings toward them. In the same way, others regard you.

Who rang the bell for Dick Whittington? Who are you ringing the bell for, and are you ringing it well?

2. God's Plans and the Cocklebur Seed

"For everything there is a season, and a time for every matter under heaven."—Eccl. 3:1

WHEN I WAS A BOY, HOW I HATED THE COCKLEBUR! AND WITH good reason, for it caused me much misery.

What is the cocklebur? It's an oval-shaped seed pod slightly more than a half inch long with scores of curving, sharp, needlelike burry hairs. Naturally, it's made that way so it will catch on passing animals (and humans) in the fall and be carried here, there, and yonder for the next year. So does Nature provide for her own.

A favorite riding place is a cow's tail. And when about a hundred or so cockleburs have managed to secure this choice spot, the cow's tail becomes a stiff, spiny club. That's why I hated the cocklebur.

For I milked four cows each morning and evening. And when they switched their tails round my bare neck, the effect was far from pleasant. How I dreaded the cocklebur season!

But just as our enemies often teach us more than our friends, so do the unpleasant, distasteful items of life give us food for thought. For the cocklebur shows how marvelously God can make his plans work despite adverse conditions.

Open the cocklebur and you find two seeds. Why two? We don't know, but we do know these two seeds are very different although they may look exactly alike. They have different sprouting schedules. One will sprout the year after it develops. The other will wait a year and sprout the second season. Why this arrangement?

Very simple. Suppose that the first sprouting season is a bad one. The bur is still tangled up in some cow's tail, or in some boy's overcoat, or the weather is too dry, or the bur gets caught too high on the grass to put its roots into the ground.

Does this mean that there will be no cocklebur plant from that seed pod? No, for the second seed still has a chance. Perhaps next year the bur will be out of the cow's tail, out of the boy's overcoat, the weather will be just right, and the bur falls down from the tall grass into nice moist soil.

Then that second seed saves the day by growing into a new cocklebur plant to make new sticky burs for cows' tails and for naughty boys to rub into girls' long hair, as they used to when I was a boy.

What a marvelous design God has for even this lowly plant!

And if he thinks so much of its welfare, how much more does he consider us, his own beloved children.

He gives us not just two chances, but many, many, many chances. He forgives us when we do wrong as often as we're sorry for our sins and ask his forgiveness.

Each day we start off with a clean slate, with minds washed fresh by sleep. Each Sunday in church we begin the week right with worship of him.

Also, the cocklebur teaches us, especially when we're young, not to give up when our aims and ambitions don't come true as we want them to. Perhaps you've already discovered that every boy and girl is different from every other boy and girl. One boy may throw a football well at ten years. Another may not do so well until he's twelve. One child learns to read well at five. Another, at six or seven.

One girl may enjoy dancing in the eighth grade. Another may not until she's in the tenth.

Don't be discouraged if you can't do certain things as well as others your age. Perhaps they can't do certain other things as well as you're doing them now. Certainly, we should all try to correct our weak points, but many young people grow discouraged too quickly because they feel inferior.

Suppose the second-year cocklebur seed saw its brother sprouting and said, "I'm no good. Look at my brother grow. What's wrong with me?" Common sense would say: "You silly thing, you're not made to sprout now. Next year your time comes."

Likewise, God made us human beings different.

Don't feel that you're inferior if your friends seem ahead of you in certain ways. *Do your best and your time will come.*

3. Dare to Be Different!

"Do not be conformed to this world but be transformed by the renewal of your mind."—Rom. 12:2

DID YOU EVER STOP TO THINK ABOUT THIS AMAZING FACT: EVERY real contribution of any great worth that has been made in this world was made by people who dared to be different?

That's a fact! No, we don't mean that they wore different clothes from their friends, or parted their hair on a different side, or had odd table manners. It's possible to be different in a queer kind of way that benefits nobody.

But all the world's great pioneers dared to be different. Daniel Boone couldn't stand civilization—so he explored Kentucky. Later on when the neighborhood in Kentucky got crowded, he pushed westward into Missouri.

Even in the world of nature the same holds true. Many years ago a Canadian applegrower noticed how one tree bore a new and lovely kind of fruit. He took cuttings from this tree and grafted them on other trees. From this one apple tree came the modern MacIntosh apple—the red, red apple with the juicy bite.

One of the dairy farmer's most reliable hay crops is alfalfa. Alfalfa is an old plant, but the kind farmers plant today—all the millions and millions of acres over the United States—is descended from a single alfalfa plant. This plant was noticed by a western farmer in a year of great drought as being the only thriving plant in the whole field. Upon investigation he discovered that its roots went deep into the earth, while its neighbors depended on the moisture in the top few inches of soil.

15

Because this single plant was different, alfalfa fields all over our land are greener and more productive.

Plants are different through no effort or courage on their part. But human beings must be different through enormous will power and thought.

King Saul tried to force his heavy armor on the shepherd boy David. But David resisted this protection so unnatural to him and went out and slew Goliath with the weapon he knew best—the slingshot.

Young Daniel and his three friends were urged to eat the rich diet from the table of King Nebuchadnezzar. But Daniel knew that simple food was best for the human body. Because he dared to be different, he was made adviser to the king.

The ancient prophet Amos saw his fellow countrymen, the Israelites, buying one another as slaves. All around he witnessed terrible injustice, with the rich oppressing the poor. Nobody else raised a voice—but Amos did. Because he dared to be different, we have his mighty words still with us—recorded in the book of Amos in the Old Testament. Men of courage still read them for inspiration.

Jesus Christ was tempted to use force, raise an army, and drive out the Romans and their cruel occupation army from his land of Israel. All his nation yearned for liberty. But Jesus knew that force would only produce more violence. He dared to be different and proclaimed the law of love—that we should love God and our fellow man and forgive our enemies. He was so different that he was crucified.

If in your heart you know that being like the crowd is wrong, dare to be different. It's not easy. And you may not succeed. But God will be with you. Trust in him. Pray and ask him for strength. When tempted to go along in acts you know are wrong, be different. Perhaps others will follow you. And even if not, dare to be different.

16

4. A Pot of Gold in an Old Field

"The kingdom of heaven is like treasure hidden in a field, which a man found and covered up; then in his joy he goes and sells all that he has and buys that field."—Matt. 13:44

LET'S PUT ON OUR THINKING CAPS AND GO WITH JESUS ON A VERY exciting treasure hunt. You read of it in the Gospel of Matthew, thirteenth chapter, verse forty-four. There our Savior tells of a man who found a treasure hidden in a field and who bought that field to get the treasure by first selling all he had to get the necessary money.

Jesus sketches the story in just a few words. Let's read between the lines and imagine what must have happened.

Even two thousand years ago, when Jesus lived, his home country of Palestine was an old, old part of the world. For several thousand years various nations had come and gone— each group conquering its predecessors. We know now that this very country was one of the first to have villages and cities.

Kings had lived and died. Whole tribes had perished or been taken captive to foreign lands, never to return—men, women, and children alike. By Jesus' time most of the towns and cities that had prospered centuries before had been forgotten, their very names and locations no longer known.

Because Palestine was, and still is, located on the main route between Africa and Asia, army after army swept through. Its people never knew what terrible conqueror would come next.

Even in peacetime keeping money secure was a problem. No banks existed, as we know them, with their huge steel vaults. Paper money and checks hadn't been thought of. All money then was either gold, silver, or copper. Or a person might invest in diamonds or other precious jewels whose value would not change.

But where could a rich man, or even a poor man, keep such treasures? Only kings and very wealthy people could have armed guards to protect them.

So people who had gold, silver, or copper money or who had

17

precious jewels had to either hide them in the house somewhere or go out on a dark night, dig a hole in the ground, and bury their treasures.

This went on for centuries. Especially in times of great danger, such as wars, did people bury their money. Of course many such treasure owners were killed, taken away as slaves to distant lands, or died of famine and disease. With them went the secrets of their hidden treasures.

We know this happened, for we still find such treasures in Palestine. The soil and climate, being dry, have helped preserve them all these many centuries.

Let's imagine that in the year 586 B.C., the year the Babylonians took Jerusalem and carried away its rich temple treasures, a man named Helon, living a few miles away, hid about two feet under the ground an earthen pitcher containing two hundred pieces of gold. Helon, with his friends, was taken to Babylon, one thousand miles to the east. He never returned, though right up until his death he always dreamed of going back for his treasure. However, being a slave, he couldn't.

Centuries passed. Helon was forgotten. Even his family never returned home. But the two hundred pieces of gold remained, only barely tarnished by the elements.

One day over six hundred years later a poor tenant farmer named ben Korah was wearily plowing in the same field once owned by the now forgotten Helon. His poor ox could barely pull even the crude wooden plow that scratched just the top few inches of soil. All his life ben Korah had known nothing but poverty and hard work. By immense toil he had managed to buy a modest home and a few decent clothes for his wife and children. He himself always went barefooted.

As he plodded away behind his ox and plow, the plow suddenly struck what ben Korah thought was a stone. For the field was full of stones, large and small. As he yanked the plow up-

18

ward to start the furrow anew, he happened to look down. No, it couldn't be!

He looked again. Yes, it was! The plow had broken into an ancient earthen pitcher. And inside, with some spilled out into the plowed soil, were handfuls of gold coins! More money right there than ben Korah had ever made or would make in his whole life.

Hastily he looked around. Nobody was in sight. He stooped down quickly and covered the pitcher again with earth. Controlling his feelings as much as he could, he continued plowing, but his mind was whirling with a thousand thoughts.

The field was not his. He was a poor man. If he stole the gold out at night, the rich landowner would surely find out and have him sold into slavery.

No, there must be a better way. Buy the land! That's it! Buy the land! Then the treasure would be his! A whole new life would open up for him and his family.

But how? He had no cash. But he did have a home. And his wife and children had a few clothes, toys, and some rather poor jewelry. They would bring enough to buy the quarter-acre containing the gold.

Ben Korah forced himself to continue plowing all day. To quit and show any abnormal excitement would arouse suspicion.

That night after the children were asleep, he announced his plans to his wife, never telling just *why* he needed the money.

My, but what she told him! Was he out of his head? Here, they had just paid for their home—she had the first decent clothes she'd ever worn—and besides, her husband wouldn't even tell her, his own wife. why he wanted the money.

Ben Korah pleaded with her to trust him. After several hours of crying she finally consented.

The next day he did sell the house. He sold his wife's clothing, leaving her only a single ragged dress. He sold his children's clothing, leaving them in the skimpiest of rags. He sold his ox and plow. He sold everything he and his family owned except their very bodies. He even sold his wife's few kitchen utensils.

Then ben Korah went to a land broker, one who buys and sells land for other people. Today we call them real-estate dealers. He told him which piece of land he wanted. He did not dare approach the actual owner, his landlord. He asked the broker not to reveal his name.

By nightfall he owned the quarter-acre, with the transfer papers signed, sealed, and delivered to him. Then he told his wife. She still thought he was crazy. Just after dark he took her to their newly bought plot of ground.

Carefully locating the exact spot, he stooped down, dug with his bare hands, for he had sold his own shovel, and brought up a fist full of gold. His wife's eyes nearly popped out of her head as the old coins glinted in the feeble lamp rays. They hastily put the money into the cloth bag they had brought for the purpose. They returned home for their last night in their old house—rich people.

We'll stop our imagining there, although it might be pleasant to imagine how this poor tenant farmer and his family now had a life of decency and comfort, and we'll go back to Jesus' statement in Matthew.

He said: "The kingdom of heaven is like treasure hidden in a field, which a man found and covered up; then in his joy he goes and sells all that he has and buys that field."

Jesus was saying: we must put God first. We must be willing to sacrifice anything we have for him. Not until we do that are we ready for heaven.

But once being willing to give God everything, we are no longer poor but rich. In return we have everything worth having. This is a strange condition for entering heaven.

God's will for us is a great treasure. What are we willing to
20

give up to find it? That answer depends on us, just as the man of Jesus' day had to decide whether he would continue to be poor or sell all he had and become rich.

5. God Is Busy in the Winter Too

> "*By the breath of God ice is given,
> and the broad waters are frozen fast.*"
> —Job 37:10

MANY BIRDS MIGRATE SOUTH TO ESCAPE THE COLD. MANY people go to Florida from the North for the same reason.

What is God doing in the frozen North from December to April? Obviously he puts many of his creatures to bed—such as the bear. They snooze away week upon week, rousing now and then to get in a more comfortable position.

From all appearances much of nature might be completely frozen. But not so.

Under many ice-covered streams water still flows. Beneath heavy sheets of ice, often two feet thick, on the lakes, the whole fish world goes about its business unless interrupted by fishermen.

Despite the apparent inactivity about woods, fields, and streams God is very busy preparing for spring and summer.

First, there is the important question of water supply for the next growing season. It is during the winter that the deep levels of water supply are put in. Winter rains and melting snows sink slowly downward. Next spring plants will send their thirsty roots deep to bring this moisture back. Also, by a mysterious process we call "capillary action" this same water will come upward to be used by shallow-rooted plants. Unless a sufficient supply of water falls and sinks in the form of rain or snow, farmers will have hard, cloddy ground to plow in the spring, and seeds won't sprout for lack of moisture.

Above ground in bushes and trees millions upon millions of tiny buds are preparing for their sudden burst when warm weather comes. They may look dead with their scaly crust. But this is only their winter overcoat, specially fitted to prevent moisture from entering, freezing, and splitting the precious bud. Slowly but surely the bud inside is maturing—dividing and subdividing itself. Comes spring and warm weather—and presto—like magic—these buds appear from nowhere.

So dreary does the landscape look in winter sometimes that we might imagine that God has deserted the world. The ancient Norsemen called cold "evil" and the sun "good." The return of spring signified to them the triumph of good over evil. Their winters were so long and hard you really couldn't blame them for this false belief. Besides, they hadn't been told of the one true God.

But winter and summer, cold and warmth, sleep and activity—all these are part of God's plan. Because of the cold season plants grow sturdier. Frost action on plowed ground breaks up clods and makes fields just right for seed growth.

In our own lives good often comes disguised as evil or in some form we find unpleasant. Boys and girls yearn for the day when they will be great leaders—when they can show to the world what they believe and what they can do. They find waiting hard. They want to grow up faster than Father Time will allow.

But now while you're young is just the right time to lay up rich treasures of a strong body, a well-trained mind, solid habits of work, worship, and play. Then, someday in due time these will all come to the surface. The better you live now, the finer adult you will be. Just as God works with nature all winter, so he prepares you now for some great work in the future.

6. What Can I Do for You?

"So whatever you wish that men would do to you, do so to them; for this is the law and the prophets."—Matt. 7:12

THESE ARE THE WORDS YOU'RE ASKED WHEN YOU ENTER A STORE: "What can I do for you?" Or you may hear this question spoken by a clerk, "May I help you?"

We can learn much from these two questions. For in a way they can represent our whole viewpoint on life.

Every boy and girl must ask this question of themselves: What can I do for the world?

This question breaks down into further questions such as: What talents and personal gifts do I have that the world needs? How can I serve God and my fellow men? What training must I have to prepare myself for the greatest service possible? Every young person should think seriously of the right answers.

Not long ago I heard a family moving to a new community. In looking around for a church to attend, they asked themselves: Which church offers us the most? Where can we get the most?

They had the shoe on the wrong foot, for as Christians they should say: In what church can we give ourselves the most?

Whatever good we have in the world today is because somebody chose to ask the question What can I give? instead of What can I get?

God gives us our bodies, brains, personalities, and personal talents to use for him and his other human children. Or rather, we are loaned them for the span of our lifetime. They don't belong to us at all.

Each person must decide for himself which questions are the most important and then decide how these questions shall be answered.

Jesus warned us against trying to get much and give little. He left no doubt as to our final fate. He told us: "Whoever would save his life will lose it." Those who live selfishly and push only their own interests come out the losers.

23

But Jesus also told us: "Whoever loses his life for my sake will find it." Those who give their lives, or rather, live for God will wind up with more than they started with.

Jesus' words seem just the opposite of what the world teaches. But who is right—Jesus Christ the Son of God or those whose advice we know cannot be trusted? Since we have only one life to live, deciding this is terribly important, too.

How much can I squeeze out of life with the least effort and sacrifice? How can I use other people for my own benefit? How can I avoid giving any money away? How can I do as little for others as possible? The non-Christian asks these questions.

What can I give? How can I serve God and man the best? What training do I need to develop my personal talents the fullest? How shall I spend my money to make it do the most good? The Christian asks these questions.

What questions we ask ourselves and the answers we give involve a priceless reward—our souls. Jesus said: "What can a man give in exchange for his own soul?"

What can I give? Ask yourself this question.

7. A New Year and a Clean Slate

(A New Year's Thought)

"Get yourselves a new heart and a new spirit!"—Ezek. 18:31

DID YOU MAKE ANY NEW YEAR'S RESOLUTIONS? IF NOT, THERE'S still time for at least one or two.

We don't know whether God keeps a calendar or not. The Bible says that his reckoning of time is different from ours. A thousand years are as a day with the Lord and a day as a thousand years. Does God have a New Year or not? For that answer we must wait.

But we do know this. God is always ready to help us start all over again in life, and at New Year's time we start the year all over. One big fact Jesus revealed about our heavenly Father is his willingness to give us another chance. Every day, not every year, but every day and even every moment he is ready to forgive our sins if we forgive others and if we ask for pardon.

Before writing paper was so cheap and plentiful, school pupils used a piece of flat, smoothly polished slate for writing. Usually these thin sheets of stone, for that's what they were, had a wooden frame for case of handling. When the slate was filled with pencil marks, the pupil wiped it clean with a damp cloth, or lacking that, with his dampened fingers. That's the way our great-great-grandparents did their homework.

From this piece of school equipment came the expression "Start off with a clean slate."

When God forgives us, he "wipes the slate clean." He removes from our hearts and minds the smudges of sin, bad thoughts, and ugly feelings. Nothing remains.

Have you ever had a bad quarrel or fight with your best friend? After a few days or hours you both felt so badly you made up and were better friends than before. Remember how good you felt inside when things where all right again? Your friendship had a "clean slate," so to speak. The bad feelings had been erased.

New Year's season is a good time to begin with a clean slate—to start over inside with new habits replacing the old. It's a good time to stop lazy practices of study and start more sensible ones. A good time to stop eating too many sweets. A good time to start obeying your parents promptly and not after much coaxing. A good time to start arriving on time at Sunday school and church.

A good time to become friendly with some lonely child in school or that timid new boy or girl just recently moved into town or the neighborhood.

A good time to start reading the Bible each day and praying to God each night.

God has provided in a wonderful way a clean slate each morning. We fall asleep each night with our bodies and brains tired from work and play. Our eyelids couldn't stay open much longer. Chemical poisons make our muscles fatigued.

Each morning we woke up refreshed—the cobwebs wiped from our minds and our muscles ready for the day. In only eight or ten hours God has in his mysterious way truly renewed our bodies.

Likewise, he can renew our souls if we want him to. That is even a greater miracle, for it involves our desire to be renewed. We must ask him to do it.

New Year's is a logical time to begin all over. Ask God to help you start the best and most wonderful year of your life.

8. A Crumbling Castle and a Wasted Life

> *"And the rain fell, and the floods came, and the winds blew and beat against that house, and it fell; and great was the fall of it"*—Matt. 7:27

ON HEART ISLAND, ONE OF THE THOUSAND ISLANDS IN THE ST. Lawrence River, in sight of the New York state mainland is a huge castle now tumbling into a state of decay.

It looks for all the world like a medieval castle on the Rhine, for that's what it was built to resemble. Let's go back into the history of this strange pile of stone looking so odd there in the St. Lawrence River.

George C. Boldt came to America from Germany as a small boy. He rose to be a millionaire many times over and once owned the Waldorf-Astoria Hotel in New York.

He loved his wife so much that he decided to erect a castle

26

and showplace that would stand as a permanent monument to her. To honor her properly, he would build a castle! And a castle like the ones on the Rhine River in Germany that he had admired as a boy.

Nothing but the best would go into this castle. He hired the best architects and artists. Hand-carved marble fireplaces made in Italy were ordered. From the Old World came mosaics, carvings, tapestries, and sculpture. The best of workmen, mural painters, landscape gardeners, masons, and carpenters came from all over the world. Money was poured out without stint to honor Mrs. Boldt.

When the castle was nearly finished, Mrs. Boldt died. The whole reason for the castle was gone. Mr. Boldt ordered the work stopped. Not another nail was driven or stone laid.

Today visitors can see cut stones lying uncrated; expensive carved woods still in their packing cases lean against the walls, with careless passers-by free to write their names on them in lipstick or crayon. Certain parts of the castle are so deteriorated that it's too dangerous to enter. Before many years go by, the building will have to be closed to the public because of the danger, and Boldt Castle will be viewed only from the outside and by those passing by in their boats on the St. Lawrence River.

What a great tribute to one man's wife! But what an awful waste!

For the same amount of money George C. Boldt could have built and equipped a full-scale college, complete with dormitories, library, dining hall, and chapel. Or he could have erected a hospital. Or set up a rotating loan fund to help needy students attend college. And he could have named these things after his wife. She would live forever in the hearts of the public. Wouldn't *Boldt College* be more to her credit than *Boldt Castle?*

27

Now few of us have millions of dollars to squander. But we do have treasures more precious.

We have our own lives, given to us by God—with our bodies, brains, personalities, abilities, aim, dreams, and ambitions. What will we do with them—build foolish life castles for succeeding generations to disrespect and make fun of or build lives that will be honored and useful?

Jesus had three great temptations to use his life foolishly and selfishly. He rejected all three. Today he calls to us and challenges us to use the great treasure of our life for him and God. How will you spend your millions?

9. Who Killed Cock Robin?

"Be kind to one another, tenderhearted, forgiving one another, as God in Christ forgave you."—Eph. 4:32

WHO KILLED COCK ROBIN? THIS IS HISTORY'S MOST FAMOUS murder case, and it was quickly solved by a confession by the murderer:

> "I," said the Sparrow,
> "With my bow and arrow."

Not every murder case is so simple, as you well know from watching television and reading comic books.

Here I shall discuss another type of killing, one not so serious as far as the law is concerned, but a very real kind. As far as I know, nobody was ever sentenced to jail for this type or even arrested. But it goes on all the time.

It's the killing of one another's feelings, especially our better kind of feelings.

Did you ever want to do something you felt was right and

28

then didn't because you feared what people would say? Or you thought, "Somebody might laugh at me." And you refrained from doing some act of kindness or courage you knew later you should have done.

Have you ever joined with the other kids in poking fun at some boy for being different? Maybe he dressed poorly because his parents didn't have enough money. Or his mother didn't care how he went to school, or whether his face was washed or not, or if his clothes were mended and neat. I have seen feelings murdered in this manner.

Once I knew a family of six children. The father was in the state prison. Neither the mother nor the children were to blame. But neighbor parents forbade their children to play with these six. By so doing they were helping to start these innocent children off to a life of crime. Nothing makes boys and girls become bad more quickly than being called bad repeatedly. These neighbors were doing everything they could to kill the best feelings inside those six children.

Boys know the quickest way to force their chums into harmful pranks and even into breaking the law. The word "chicken" is all it takes to break their will power. It takes a boy with a strong backbone to resist the word "chicken."

Abraham Lincoln once said he never stepped rudely on anybody else as he rose to become President. That is, he never did cruel or unfair acts or used false words to deride his opponents. Not every man is so fair—nor so great—as Abraham Lincoln. No wonder he is loved the whole world over. No man was ever more manly, honest, or more kindly.

A verse in the Bible goes well here. "Be kind to one another."

Much of what we see in the world seems to say: "Be cruel to one another."

If this one Bible verse were said every day by every Christian and truly followed, what different people we would have! Say it to yourself—"Be kind to one another."

29

Don't commit this type of murder, for if you do, you also kill some very fine feelings of your own. Don't let cruelty replace kindness as the guide for your conduct.

The Bible has another verse that warns us: "Whatever a man sows, that he will also reap." If we sow kindness, we receive kindness back. If we are cruel, cruelty will come back to us.

"Be kind to one another."

10. What Are Good Manners Good for?

"Love one another with brotherly affection; outdo one another in showing honor"—Rom. 12:10

WHAT DOES THE TERM "GOOD MANNERS" MEAN?

The word "manner" means *the way we do something.*

For example, when we want a piece of bread at the table, in what way do we get it? Do we say, "I want a piece of bread," or, "Would you please pass the bread?" The latter is the correct way.

We usually regard courtesy, good manners, and politeness only as the way we treat other people. But our actions have a funny way of coming right back home. For by and large, other people treat us the same way we treat them; at least I have found it so.

Consequently, the way we treat others is the way we must expect to be treated. Good manners toward others means good manners toward ourselves.

One very old guide to good manners goes like this:

> The correct thing to do and say;
> Is the kindest thing in the kindest way.

If you don't know all the rules of good manners, think, act,
30

and treat others with kindness and consideration. Kindness and consideration are hard to hide. Those around us soon know that we wish them well even if we can't remember all the rules of good manners.

True good manners come from a kind heart.

But even the kindest heart needs training in common, everyday courtesies.

Here are some key words to memorize in your lesson on good manners. They are short, simple, and won't use much breath in saying them. Yet they reap dividends. They are:

"Thank you."

"Pardon me."

"If you please."

"Allow me to help you."

We could name many more such short phrases. The wonder is that even these few are so badly neglected. In a day when there is so much talk going on, these few key phrases, which unlock such magical doors, lie unused on our brain's shelf collecting dust.

Somebody has called courtesy, or good manners, the oil that lubricates human society. Oil is essential to machinery. It doesn't do any work but keeps the metal parts in a machine from rubbing against one another and burning up or wearing out.

Courtesy does the same for people. And just as oil is absolutely essential to machinery, good manners and courtesy are necessary for human beings.

Even three-year-old children can learn to say "Thank you" and "Please." I have heard them.

Do you want to receive courtesy from others? Then, be courteous to them.

11. The Magic Mirror

"Judge not, and you will not be judged."—Luke 6:37

LET ME TELL YOU ABOUT A MAGIC MIRROR. IT ISN'T MADE OF glass and quicksilver, like the ordinary mirror. Nor is it made of crystal.

You can't buy it in a store or manufacture it with any known material. This mirror moves around. It belongs to other people, yet you have full use of it constantly.

This magic mirror is the other person's face.

Yes, believe it or not but you can tell what you are like by looking at other people's faces.

No, you can't see how big your nose is or how many freckles or moles or warts you have on your face. Nor if your cheeks are rosy or pale.

But you can tell about the important things—whether or not your face is frowning or smiling or sad or happy or bold or shy or confident or afraid or selfish or generous. Somehow our inner feelings show on our faces.

And by some magic what we show on our faces gets written on our friends' faces too. I know a boy who is shy. He is so shy other people think he's actually unfriendly. Of course he isn't. But his face looks like he's unfriendly. So other people, seeing his face, say to themselves, "This boy is cold and unfriendly. If he wants to be that way, I will be that way too." And all the time the boy wonders why other people shy away from him. They look at his face, that's all. If he could only realize it, he could see how his face looks by looking at theirs. If he could only force his face to be friendly and smiling, their faces would change too.

Jesus must have had a face that showed his feelings. It was a sincere face. Children were attracted to him. They saw how he loved them.

People in trouble, poor people, sick people, cripple people, blind people, paralyzed people, people with leprosy and epilepsy and all sorts of diseases, wicked people who were sorry for their sins—in fact any kind at all who longed for help and forgiveness—saw in his face a great Friend. Because his face shone with such great kindness and strength, in return their faces were changed too.

But for cruel and hard people he had another face—one of great sternness. He told them they were wrong and that they must change. They disliked him so much they finally crucified him.

Painters and sculptors have had great difficulty trying to paint and carve Jesus' face—so full of compassion and strength and goodness was it. Leonardo da Vinci, who painted the famous "Last Supper" scene, searched for many years for a man whose face could serve as a model for Christ.

I cannot guarantee that this magic mirror will work perfectly every time. Sometimes people do not respond as they should or as we want them too. Even Jesus with all his great works and love was misunderstood. But that didn't cause him to abandon his own way of thinking and doing.

If your face expresses love for others, consideration, courage, cheerfulness, and confidence, you will be surprised how those you meet have the same kind of attitude.

12. The Little Pond That Got Fresh

> "Give, and it will be given to you; good measure, pressed down, shaken together, running over. . . ."—Luke 6:38

ONCE THERE WAS A VERY UNHAPPY LITTLE POND OF WATER. IT was unhappy because it hated to give away any of itself. For it was a selfish little pond.

It was located in a small valley through which ran a tiny stream. Some farmer in years past had built a small earthen

33

dam and caused the water to back up a few yards, thus creating the little pond.

The pond, being a selfish and foolish pond, did not stop to think that it existed only because a stream ran into it on the upper side. It thought only of the water it lost over the spillway at the other end. To see this water, even though it was a small amount, running on downhill caused it to be very unhappy.

"If there was only some way to keep all this water," it said to itself, "then I could be much deeper, perhaps the deepest pond in the whole countryside."

Finally it hit upon a plan: "I'll stop the spillway! Then no more water can drain out. That's the way!"

So it concentrated on the grass and weeds that grew along the spillway. Soon the vegetation was so thick and high that no water could escape. It rose higher and higher, inch by inch.

Terrible things happened below, in the next field, and the next, and the next. The cattle and sheep and horses that depended on the tiny stream flowing through the pond now had no water. Their masters had to haul water for the poor thirsty beasts.

The fishes, tadpoles, and frogs in the stream below all died.

You might think that all this suffering would make the selfish pond change its mind and open the spillway—but no! Not on your life. For being a selfish pond, it thought only of itself.

But soon a change occurred that was not a pleasant one. Thick, slimy green stuff appeared on the pond's surface. It never had that trouble before. Also, boys and girls quit swimming in the pond. Not that the pond liked children, but it liked the news and chatter they brought along. The pond was very proud of the raft they had built out in the middle that was now unused. One day the pond was cut to the quick when it

34

heard a boy, standing on the bank, say, "This old pond smells bad. I don't like it any more!"

That night the little pond did some very serious thinking. It saw what a selfish, foolish pond it had been and how impossible it was just to add to one's own size without causing some suffering and finally your own unhappiness.

The next morning it asked the weeds and grass that had been clogging up the spillway to move over. Then the top water gushed out—down the hill, filling the dried-up stream bed. Along with the surface water went all the slimy green stuff. Once more the pond sparkled clear and clean in the sunlight. Not only did it look different—it *felt* different. Within a few days there were dozens and dozens of boys and girls splashing and playing around. And you never saw a happier little pond in your life!

It had learned what every pond and lake must know: *It is the surface water you give away that makes you clean and beautiful.* If you keep it all to yourself, you get stale and ugly.

13. God Has a Purpose for You and Me

"And Jesus said to them, 'Follow me and I will make you become fishers of men.' "—Mark 1:17

HAVE YOU EVER FELT LIKE SAYING, "I'M NO GOOD. WHAT COULD anybody see in me, anyway?"

You would be surprised to learn how many people, grownups as well as boys and girls, feel that they're here but just what they're here for they couldn't tell for a million dollars. They know they were born, they know they're alive, but just what for is something they couldn't say.

At times we all feel like we're good for nothing or that nobody loves us. But our feelings couldn't be further from the

35

truth. For God, who made us, has a purpose for us. Just as a carpenter who makes a house intends that people should live in it, God made us for some specific use.

We are slowly realizing that God wastes nothing in the creation process. Even the most obnoxious or ugly and unattractive parts of his creation can be useful.

Somebody said, "Weeds are plants we haven't found a use for yet." The castor-bean plant is a big, ungainly weed. When I was a boy, I hoed them from our cornfield. They were a nuisance. But castor-bean oil makes very fine medicine and the best lubricating oil for highspeed airplane engines.

The tomato is our most widely used vegetable in America. None other comes near it in amount raised and used. Think of the tomato catsup, tomato soup, tomato juice, tomato paste, spaghetti sauce, and the many other ways we eat tomatoes besides that most delicious way—raw. How we'd hate to give up tomatoes! But not many years ago we regarded the tomato plant as a decoration only. My mother used to tell me how people thought the tomato poisonous when she was a small girl! Imagine!

Seventy-five years ago cotton ginners threw cotton seeds outside their gins where the fiber was separated from the seed. Only enough was saved for the next year's crop. Along came cattle and ate the delicious seed. Being rather stupid creatures and loving the cotton seed so much, they ate until they were gorged and finally died. People said, "Cotton seeds are poisonous for cattle. Keep them away!"

Then somebody discovered the truth. Today cotton seed provides hundreds of fine products, including very fine and expensive food for livestock—cottonseed cake and cottonseed meal. Oil, pressed from the seed, is fine-grade cooking oil for our kitchens and for salad mixes.

We could fill a whole book with such examples from nature and science, but let's turn to people.

God has a purpose for every human being. Each person, no matter how rich or poor, no matter what his or her color or race or nation or religion, has something good to contribute to the world. That includes you and me.

The famous singer Marian Anderson was a Negro girl from Philadelphia with no influential friends. People saw possibilities in her and encouraged her singing. Today millions thrill to her voice. Throughout Asia colored people listen to her interpretations of America.

Men said about Jesus Christ, "He is no good. He is dangerous. Let us kill him." But God's purpose for his Son could not be thwarted by evil. Jesus himself said:

> The stone which the builders rejected
> has become the chief cornerstone.

He was referring to the way his life and way would become victorious.

What is God's purpose for your life? That is for you to find out, if you haven't already. But this much never doubt: *He has a purpose for you.*

14. God Loves Even His Ugly Creatures

"And God saw everything that he had made, and behold, it was very good."—Gen. 1:31

HOW COULD ANYBODY LOVE THE HORRIBLE-LOOKING DEEP-SEA creatures, those with rows upon rows of teeth, and bulging eyes, and monstrous plated scales?

How could a person think that a cruel crocodile or his wily cousin, the alligator, could be attractive? And think of the poisonous serpents. Not to mention the thousands of kinds of

37

insects that sting and bite us and eat up our crops and clothing and even undermine our homes.

Does anybody look upon these creatures as being anything but horrible and utterly useless?

Yes, God does. For he created each of them with infinite care.

In the Bible in the first chapter of Genesis, the thirty-first verse, we see what God, the Creator, really thinks of all his creations: "And God saw everything that he had made, and behold, it was very good."

Furthermore, God loves his human children, too, even those whom we think unattractive, just as much as he loves us.

He created people of white, yellow, brown, red, and black skins and all kinds of mixtures. One color or race might think another unattractive, But not God.

And within our own races there are individuals whose very appearance is unattractive to us. Some have very homely faces —at least to us. But they are still God's children.

But worse than unattractive face or body is ugly conduct. When we do wrong, even terribly wrong, somebody still loves us. That somebody is God.

Think of the worst, meanest, most cruel individual you can. Now ask yourself this question: Does God love that person?

The answer that comes from Christ is: Yes, he does. In fact God so loves that person that he sent his only begotten Son to earth. God loves him so much that if he believes on Christ, he will have everlasting life.

How unbelievable!

No, God doesn't love that person's sins and misconduct. He wants him to turn from his bad ways and be a Christian. But the person himself he does love, just as our parents may love us but not like at all our misconduct.

Jesus prayed even for the wicked men who were crucifying him. Among his last words on the cross were "Father, forgive them; for they know not what they do." So great was his love even for his enemies that he prayed this prayer.

We human beings cannot completely understand God's love even for the worst of evildoers. We simply must accept it and try to imitate God. And this love of his can do more than anything else in the whole world to make good people out of bad people. Nothing else is so strong as this invisible force we call the love of God.

No, not punishment or war or atom or hydrogen bombs or fear or strength of muscles can accomplish what the love of God can and does accomplish.

God loves even his worst children. And that includes us, too, when we are at our worst.

15. Why Should We Tell About Jesus?

"And Jesus came and said to them, . . . Go therefore and make disciples of all nations, baptizing them in the name of the Father and of the Son and of the Holy Spirit."
—Matt. 28:18-19

FROM THE DAY JESUS ROSE FROM THE DEAD ALMOST TWO thousand years ago, his followers have all done this: They have gone about telling others about him.

Imagine this impossible situation: Upon seeing the empty tomb that first bright Easter day, the two Marys and the disciples who were there kept completely silent. Nobody would ever have known!

But the angel guarding the tomb said, "Go tell others." And they did. They ran to tell the glad news that Jesus, their Master, was risen. At first even the apostles didn't believe, thinking it an idle tale. But this truth, like all others, proved itself.

39

And ever since, men and women all over the globe have been telling about Jesus. The story will never stop.

In songs we call hymns, in the Bible, in sermons, in Sunday schools, colleges, universities, hospitals, and in a thousand other ways the story of Jesus is repeated.

And like the apostles, many do not believe at first. Some never do.

Strangely enough, thousands have volunteered to leave their native countries and journey to distant, dangerous places to tell savage tribes of God's great love for them as revealed through Christ. David Livingstone did just this. He educated himself to become a missionary to China on the other side of the earth. When a war prevented this, he chose to go to Africa. He finally died in the jungles after years of witnessing for Christ. Why did he do this? Because Jesus meant so much to him, he simply *had* to tell those who had never heard. Nobody made him go. He wanted to.

When we like something, we tell others, don't we? A new car, a thrilling television program, a new family in the neighborhood, a big new fire engine, or a basketball game in which the home team wins by one point in the last ten seconds—we quickly tell about these.

But all these are nothing in importance compared to Jesus Christ. Yet how few of us ever mention him to another person? Have you ever invited a boy or girl to attend Sunday school and church with you? You could do them no greater favor.

Imagine this situation: Suppose it were suddenly against the law to mention Jesus' name or what he did or who he was. No Sunday school next Sunday. No singing in church. No sermon by the minister. No television programs or movies about Christ. And suppose we all obeyed this foolish law. How quickly we would miss the message of Jesus!

Naturally this law is impossible. But many good Americans act as if it did exist. They never tell of Christ, and they never listen to anybody else tell of him. And their lives are poorer for it.

To Jesus Christ we owe so much. As wicked as the world is today, it would be far worse had Christ not come. He is the hope of the world. And the more people who hear of him and accept him as their Savior, the better the world will be.

Our church's missionary program, with its ministers, and nurses, and doctors, and agricultural experts, and all the others who give their lives to tell of Christ in the far corners of the earth, needs our money and our prayers.

And if we can't be a missionary in a foreign nation, Jesus expects us to tell of him right here. Some will listen. Some will not. And if we tell of him, Christ will reward us.

16. Are the Great Heroes All Dead?

"He who believes in me will also do the works that I do; and greater works than these will he do."—John 14:12

MOST OF THE HEROES WE READ ABOUT ARE DEAD. THEIR SPIRIT, their courage, and their thrilling exploits live on. We read about them, but they themselves are no longer with us.

Name them off—Roland, the great Frank who died at the hand of the Saracens; St. George of England, who slew the dragon; Beowulf, who conquered the evil Grendel; Hector of Troy; Ulysses the Greek; David, the shepherd boy who killed the giant Goliath; the apostle Paul, who died in Rome for Jesus Christ; George Washington, the father of our country; Robert Scott, who died in the bleak Antarctic returning from the South Pole; Magellan, who commanded the first ships to circle the earth but who died in the Philippines.

I could name dozens and dozens of others you'd recognize instantly and whose exploits thrill us still after all these years.

But are all the great heroes dead? No, some haven't even been born yet. And many haven't grown up. Right now some future hero is five, six, seven, eight, nine, ten, eleven, twelve, thirteen, fourteen, fifteen, or sixteen years old or older. Today some future hero who will do great things for mankind is in kindergarten.

Heroes of the future will be different from those in the past. At least in some ways. But the same qualities of daring, imagination, and adventure will be required. The frontiers to conquer may be of a different kind, perhaps harder.

For example, one dangerous frontier right now is this: How shall the different races of men live in peace and learn to love one another? Dr. Martin Luther King, a Negro Baptist minister in Montgomery, Alabama, is a hero on this racial frontier. When men hated him, he loved them. When he had good reason for striking back in a tense situation, he did not.

Another great frontier is world peace. How can the different nations live on this earth without war? We know that another great war will destroy us all. What heroes of peace can have the wisdom to help prevent war? Perhaps the answer will be not one or two great heroes, but many millions of unknown people praying to God and working for peace.

The frontier of science will have heroes aplenty. How can we arrange the forces of nature to provide enough food, clothing, shelter, and medical care for all the earth's rapidly growing population? Scientific heroes are working desperately now to produce power and more food, using the God-given resources of nature.

What will these heroes be like, these new ones?

They will be daring, adventurous, willing to take risks, willing to take jobs with low pay and great danger, and they will be daring enough to stand ridicule and opposition. They must think for themselves and speak the truth in kindness but firmness. They must study how to win others. Once they are sure they are right, they must be willing to proceed at any cost to themselves.

God depends heavily on human heroes. Our greatest hero, of course, is Jesus Christ. Because of his example countless people since have been lifted up from cowardice to courage. Christ had all the qualities of a truly great hero. Study his life closely, and you will learn how to be a hero yourself.

17. The Mightiest Army in the World

> "'Therefore God has highly exalted him . . . that at the name of Jesus every knee should bow, in heaven and on earth."—Phil. 2:9-10

WHAT IS THE MIGHTIEST ARMY IN THE WORLD? AMERICAN? Russian? English? Chinese?

Is it equipped with tanks, guns, bazookas, atom bombs, H-bombs, machine guns, atomic submarines, missiles and anti-missiles, and anti-antimissiles, and anti-anti-antimissiles?

No, none of these.

It has no guns, not even a single rifle. In fact, when it starts using guns to shoot others with, it is helping defeat itself.

The mightiest army in the world is the Christian Church, composed of followers of Jesus Christ. Millions of them all over the world have pledged their loyalty to him. And many of them would gladly die for Christ rather than betray him.

This mightiest army in the world is nearly two thousand years old. Jesus started it with twelve men. He, its first leader, let men crucify him rather than fight them with force. Instead, he chose the weapon of love, the strongest force in the whole world.

He told us that God is love. If God is love, then can you defeat love? No, for you cannot defeat God.

Strangely enough, even though the early followers of Christ were often killed for the faith, more and more people joined the ranks of this strange army. Even important Roman officials gave up their jobs and positions of honor to become members.

As the army grew, selfish and evil men joined it too, hoping to profit. Some became high church officials, but even all their greed and malice couldn't overcome the Church.

Dictators, kings, czars, Caesars, princes, generals, and military marshals have tried to suppress it. They all failed. In fact they only made it stronger.

When I was a boy, we had a chinaberry tree that grew next to the fence in a back field. Each year we cut it down. But each cutting only made more sprouts the next year. We never did kill that tree.

The Church is the same way. It cannot be destroyed.

Today the Church has spread to all lands. Men of all colors and languages hail Christ as Lord and Savior. Many do not, but that is our challenge and privilege, to tell them, too, of how Christ came to the world to save every single person.

The arms the Church uses are love, persuasion, good will, acts of charity and mercy, defending the helpless, prayer, teaching, preaching, worship, and pointing out evil. These seem rather pale and weak means of gaining victory compared to the terrible arms developed by our scientists. But the arms of the Church bring life, not death.

How proud we should be to join and be a member of the Church. With all its imperfections and weaknesses caused by its members, it cannot fail.

One hymn writer has written in a great song:

> Like a mighty army
> Moves the church of God.

The same song says:

> We have Christ's own promise,
> And that cannot fail.

Aren't you proud to be a part of the mightiest army in the world?

18. The Two Little Grains of Wheat

"Truly, truly, I say to you, unless a grain of wheat falls into the earth and dies, it remains alone; but if it dies, it bears much fruit"—John 12:24

ONCE UPON A TIME TWO LITTLE GRAINS OF WHEAT GREW SIDE by side. They were both born and raised on the same "head," that is, the part of the wheat stalk that contains the seed. These two grains had over fifty brothers and sisters who were born at the same time.

The two grains were close friends. They had grown up together. Outwardly you might say they were identical twins, judging by appearances. Yet there was a world of difference between them.

One was bright, gay, and unselfish. The other was vain, proud, and self-centered, thinking that every field mouse and meadow lark that came by looked only at it.

As summer turned to fall and the frosty nights got colder, farmers began to harvest the wheat. They brought their thrashing machinery into the fields—whir-r-r-r-r-r-r-r, rattle, rattle, rattle, clackety, clack, it went—and separated all the wheat seeds from their stalks. Round and round the seeds went inside a drum at a dizzying speed, making their heads spin.

45

Then they fell into a wagon with literally tens of thousands of their wheat-seed cousins.

Shortly afterward, with millions and millions of almost identical grains they were sucked through a dark, roaring tunnel called by the farmers a suction tube. Up, up, up, into a grain elevator they were pulled by the invisible air; then they dropped from a terrible height to their winter's resting place.

By a thousand in one miracle the two little grains of wheat who had lived so closely all summer and fall found themselves now snuggled side by side also in the grain elevator. How glad they were to see each other, despite their different characters.

Outside the winter wind howled and snow fell. Inside the millions and millions of wheat seeds slept peacefully, waking now and then to whisper to one another.

One very cold day the selfish grain asked the other, "What do you think will happen to me now?"

"I don't know exactly," the other replied, "but I heard the seeds over in the corner of the bin, where they can hear the outside conversation, say that we are going to be planted. And lucky for us too. I understand that all the other elevators around contain "flour" grains. They're literally ground up into a fine powder and eaten. What a fate! It makes me shudder. Think how fortunate we are."

"I don't care about them. And why *should* we be ground up? We've never done anything to deserve it. But I still want to know what will happen to me."

The other grain patiently replied, "Let's listen to the seeds lying outside. Maybe they can tell us."

From the seeds nearest the outside they learned that "being planted" meant being placed in the ground, covered up with dirt, and later having one's beautiful brown, shiny coat split wide open by a "sprout" that came from inside.

The selfish seed began to weep.

"How horrible! How perfectly horrible. And do you realize that I was probably the loveliest seed on our entire stalk? Or in the whole field, for that matter.

"Hush now. It won't help to rave like that," whispered the unselfish seed.

"I'm *not* raving, but I *won't* sprout. I won't, I tell you!"

"They say that if you won't sprout, you die and rot and nobody remembers you. I'd think twice if I were you," said the other, trying to talk sense into its brother's head.

"I'll take my chances," it replied. "At least I *know* what I'm like now, and that's better than changing."

Soon afterward all the millions of wheat seeds in the elevator were loaded into large wagons and then with a terrifying whir-r-r-ing sound were dumped into a seed-planting machine. The selfish grain shrieked with horror, protesting all the while that it wouldn't go.

As fate would have it, the two grains fell into the ground side by side and no sooner landed than a layer of moist black dirt fell on top of them.

"Help! help!" cried the selfish grain. "Somebody get me out of here. It's dark and I'm smothering!"

"Hush now. I'm just as scared as you, but screaming won't help in the least. Our mother wheat plant must have gone through something like this, and no wheat stalk that ever grew was lovelier than she."

"I don't care! I'm different. I won't sprout. I want to get out of here! Help! Help!" screamed the selfish seed.

But that was impossible.

Under the dark, damp soil they could feel the difference between day and night. In the daytime their dark home became warm and cozy under the sun's rays. At night they nearly froze. About the third day they both awoke with splitting headaches. My, how they did hurt!

Actually their pain was quite natural. You might call them

"growing pains" they were so natural, that is, pains that some-how come to us all in the process of growing up.

Their heads felt as if they would burst. What a pain!

From what they had overheard back in the elevator, they both realized that they were about to sprout.

The selfish seed cried angrily, "I won't sprout, I tell you!"

The unselfish seed replied, "Frankly I'm not crazy about the idea myself, but it's the only way I'll ever see the sun, the trees, the lovely blue sky, or the meadow larks again. And you don't really die. You know that. You simply change form and live far more wonderfully than before. It's just being willing to give yourself up that's the hard part. Come on now, brother, we've been together so long. We were born and raised to-gether. We spent those long months together in the elevator. And now we have this glorious chance to see the world to-gether. Why don't you be sensible?"

But the other was stubborn. "I'm not committing suicide. Go ahead if you want to."

"Please."

"No," said the other, "and that's final."

"Well, here goes. Ouch! my head! Oh-o-o-o-o-o-o-o-o-o-o-o-oh! My beautiful coat is splitting. There now, it's over. I'll never be the same again. Please come, brother; it's my last chance to talk with you. Won't you give up your pride?"

But the selfish seed said No.

The freshly sprouted seed sent a lovely green shoot upward through the moist soil and peeked out at the loveliest, brightest blue sky it had ever seen. It drew on its remaining strength in-side its body to send down a tender root to draw up more food and water. Above, as its head shot higher, it saw thousands of other wheat plants, pale pastel green in color, thrusting their way upward toward the life-giving sun. Meadow larks shot past full of cheerful song.

Under the dark soil lay the poor little selfish seed, its body now dead and decaying. A worm came by and took a nibble. The rest of it became moldy and soon was a part of the soil itself.

If we could choose, which seed would we be like?

19. Step into the Magic World of Books

"And he stood up to read; and there was given to him [Jesus] the book of the prophet Isaiah."—Luke 4:16-17

WE CAN SEE ON TELEVISION THE GREAT PEOPLE OF OUR DAY— presidents, kings, princes, scientists, writers, ministers, labor leaders, and all the rest.

But what about the great leaders of the past—How can we meet them?

Very simple. There is a way available. Without your stirring from your home town, they can speak to you.

How?

Through books. Yes, through the printed page men of old come to us, speaking the great words of the world. Stirring messages, famous speeches, thrilling words known to all—they are all there between the pages of some book.

Here is Moses, one of the world's great geniuses of all times —military hero, writer, prophet, desert warrior—sitting there on Mount Sinai. Or we find him in his tent, writing far into the night—writing the Ten Commandments and other laws that we read in the Bible.

Or we see the great David, once a shepherd boy, now king in Jerusalem, writing the twenty-third psalm, which begins, "The Lord is my shepherd, I shall not want . . . ."

Or Jesus, sitting on a mountaintop, preaching to his disciples, who remembered his thrilling words and wrote them down. He started out, "Blessed are the poor in spirit . . . ." Through

49

the greatest Book, the Bible, we know even the words Jesus spoke and so many of his actions. We know how he was crucified and rose from the dead. Through the printed page we may meet the Master and Savior.

In books about early Christian heroes we read of brave actions of those who died in the Roman arenas because they would not deny Christ.

In his own words we read of Galileo's discoveries. And Copernicus.' These two men changed our whole conception about the universe.

We can read the account of Patrick Henry, the famous Virginia patriot, as he declared at the risk of his own life: "Give me liberty, or give me death!" And we read in the Declaration of Independence what our forefathers thought about liberty as they signed that great document that begins, "When in the course of human events . . . ." And later much the same group of men began the Constitution of the United States with these words, "We, the people of the United States, in order to form a more perfect Union . . . ."

Or by picking up another book and turning to the right page, we read the last words of Captain Robert Scott, the English Antarctic explorer, as he and his companions huddled together in their tiny tent just eleven miles away from safety. Together they died, but their words will thrill men for all time.

Or you may discover science, history, poetry, religion, and the world of what we call "fiction" from the printed page. How much poorer the world would be without Mark Twain's *Tom Sawyer* and *Huckleberry Finn*. Have you read them? Or who would want a world without Booth Tarkington's *Penrod* and *Penrod and Sam*?

Or suppose that every copy of Hans Christian Andersen's *Fairy Tales* were destroyed? The world would be sadder without "The Ugly Duckling" and "The Little Tin Soldier."

It was in book form that the world first met Charles Dickens'

Christmas Carol a century ago. Men will always love the story of Scrooge, Bob Cratchit, and Tiny Tim. Yet many boys and girls have never read the beloved *Christmas Carol.* Instead they use their God-given eyes to watch cheap and harmful television programs and read trashy comic books and magazines.

Have you ever read the life story of Daniel Boone, or Abraham Lincoln, or Woodrow Wilson, or Sir Alexander Fleming, or Christopher Columbus, or Louis Pasteur, or Thomas Alva Edison, or Jim Thorpe, the great Indian athlete? Why not?

Many boys and girls today say they don't have time to read. This is not so. They have much more time than boys and girls ever had in the history of the world.

It is not so much a matter of time as how we use our time. If you spend from one to four hours a day watching television, then you have little time left to read—to meet the great men and women of the world in books.

But if you choose, you can meet them all alone, there in your room or wherever you choose to close your mind to everything around, open a book, and start reading.

Practically all school learning past the fifth grade is achieved by reading. So by reading books you improve your school marks also.

Here they are, waiting for you to meet them. Right in your own school or community library are literally hundreds and hundreds of the world's great—what they did, what they said, what they wrote.

Want to know them? Just open a book.

20. A Broken Organ and a Lovely Song

(Christmas)

"Make a joyful noise to the Lord, all the lands!
Serve the Lord with gladness!
Come into his presence with singing!"—Ps. 100:1-2

HOW COULD A BROKEN CHURCH ORGAN CAUSE US TO HAVE OUR best loved Christmas carol?

In fact, how can many things that cause us inconvenience and even hardship produce our greatest blessings?

For the well-known story of the broken church organ let's go back to the year 1818 at Christmas season in the small German village of Oberndorf.

The priest of the Roman Catholic church there was discouraged. For of all the times in the year when the church organ should be working, it should be at Christmas, when so many glad and great songs are sung and when the children's choir was most active.

But big troubles can come in small packages. So it was with Joseph Mohr, the young twenty-six-year-old priest. For mice, tiny mice with sharp teeth, had gotten in the organ and eaten holes in the leather bellows that supplied air for the organ pipes. No organ music *that* Christmas.

The priest talked the situation over with his organist, Franz Grüber, also very young, only twenty-nine. They decided to write a Christmas song themselves that could be played very simply on the zither, a harplike instrument. Mohr would write the words, and Grüber would write the music.

They had only a few hours. But often we can do things when we *must* do them. So it was with them.

Perhaps God wanted a new song to tell of his Son's birth, a lovely new song saved all those centuries and now to be born in the hearts and minds of two unknown men, no better known than the disciples who followed Christ nearly two thousand years ago. But God can make us instruments of greatness if we will but open our hearts to him.

The young priest walked out under the stars. The night was so silent, so bright, so still. A holy night, it seemed.

The words shaped in his mind—silent night . . . holy night . . . all is calm . . . all is bright.

Meanwhile Franz Grüber worked on the tune. And when they came together, they changed it until it fitted the words.

And that Christmas they had a new Christmas carol about a very old story—the tale of Jesus' birth. The children loved it from the start. The older people loved it. Soon it became well known in the area. And before many years the whole world took to its heart this song caused by a broken organ.

Strangely enough this was the only tune that Franz Grüber ever had published. For shortly afterward he and his family came to America, settling in Pennsylvania. There he lived for over forty years more, dying in 1863. His one great task had been done back in Austria forty-five years before—the giving of a great, lovely song to a world that could not resist singing it.

Today the entire Christian Church loves this short, simple, and truly beautiful Christmas carol—written because some hungry, cold little mice thought a church organ was a good place to find a winter's meal and a nice place to live.

Blessings do come in strange ways. Every hardship offers some reward if we look hard enough. Every inconvenience may prove to be in our favor. With God's help even the worst experience can make us better people.

21. How God Makes His Wild Creatures Well

"Even the sparrow finds a home,
and the swallow a nest for herself,
where she may lay her young."—Ps. 84:3

WE HAVE VETERINARIANS, OR ANIMAL DOCTORS, TO TAKE OUR pets and our prize cattle and horses to when they are sick, but have you ever asked yourself who doctors the wild animals?

Somebody does, you know. God does. In his infinite loving care he has provided ways by which animals treat themselves when they are sick or injured.

Perhaps you have seen your pet cat or dog eating grass. A funny sight, yes. But they're taking medicine. Just what the grass does for them, I haven't the slightest notion, but they eat it because of some bodily craving. Grass is one of their medicines.

An old expression going back thousands of years is "A dog licking his wounds." Yes, that's what a dog does when he's cut up or bitten by other dogs or enemy animals. He licks and licks and licks the cut place in his skin with his rough tongue. Perhaps the action brings out the poisons that accumulate. Perhaps his saliva contains some kind of healing medicine. We all know, at any rate, that dogs recover from horrible wounds with no attention at all if simply left alone.

A wounded bear will go right away to a certain plant to eat leaves and bark from it. Somehow he knows they will put his body in good condition to recover.

As a boy I was impressed by the way pigs could recover from wounds that would kill a human being. They would lie in the mud and then lie in the sun. Perhaps they knew instinctively, as we all now know, that the rays of the sun kill germs and that the warmth of the sun possesses a mysterious healing power. All hospitals today own expensive electrical machines that imitate in their effects the sun's rays, thus doing for human beings what God's sunlight does for his wild creatures.

Men who have hunted much tell of animals such as deer and foxes with only three legs—the other having been shot off or caught in a steel trap and gnawed off by the poor animal itself to escape. How did they get well? God helped them, that's how.

In their eating habits, too, wild creatures keep healthy. They shun foods not good for them. Nor will they often eat too much, unlike human beings. Somehow God has given them the instinct for eating the right things in the right amounts.

Last summer I was fishing and caught a fish too small to keep. It had swallowed the hook completely, and I knew that to pull it out meant certain death for the fish. My companion, a veteran fisherman, advised, "Just cut the line. The fish won't die. The acids in its stomach will dissolve the hook in a few days, and our little friend here will be as good as new."

As the fish swam away after I cut the line near its mouth, my fishing companion turned to me and said, "Isn't it wonderful how God has given animals the power to get well from their hurts?"

Yes, it is wonderful. In fact, one of those miracles we cannot understand. In his infinite wisdom our heavenly Father provides for his wild creatures. He gives them food. He heals their wounds. He gives them skills of flight and escape. Their instincts direct them in building nests and mud houses, and digging caves against the winter's cold.

As he cares for them, God cares for us even more. With each discovery of a new medicine a new way of operating on sick people, or a new way of preventing disease God opens another door into the world of healing. Our doctors, nurses, and hospitals are dedicated to making us well and keeping us well.

Yes, God loves his wild creatures. He provides for their health.

With man's help he provides for ours too.

22. The Power of One Person

"I can do all things in him who strengthens me."
—Phil. 4:13

YOU WOULD THINK THAT IN SUCH A BIG WORLD WITH SO MANY people one person would have very little influence, wouldn't you?

Well, you couldn't be more wrong.

For just one person can have a great deal of influence. And don't forget it!

For today when we have such big cities, schools, armies, and even such big churches, we think that just bigness counts. Well, God doesn't think so. And if he doesn't, we shouldn't.

Just one person thinking rightly and acting bravely has usually been the reason why these big organizations can live at all.

Just one man voting the right way saved the United States from having Aaron Burr as President of the United States. What a terrible thing that would have been, as you know if you've read American history at all.

Just one United States Senator, voting according to his conscience, saved President Andrew Johnson, who succeeded Abraham Lincoln, from being cast out of office. We know now that this one senator was right, but at the time he was hounded, had terrible things said about him, and was never able to win another election again. Just one man saved our nation from doing a disgraceful thing.

Because we hear so much of brave, great, and brilliant people, we start thinking that such persons as ourselves don't count.

Nothing is further from the truth. God depends on us—on you and me—for some specific task. Nobody else can or will do this one job. What job is it? I cannot say for you, but I can say for myself. I know there are certain tasks that, if I don't do, don't get done, and the world is just that much worse off.

Every day in some school a boy's or girl's feelings are hurt by cruel words. What brave boy or girl will stand up for them?

In every church ministers and Sunday-school teachers need help in their important jobs. Who will help them?

Right now there are sick people lying in hospitals neglected because of lack of trained nurses. Who will be the nurses of the future?

Our nation needs many thousands of high-school teachers, especially men teachers. Boys are actually going to jail because of lack of good, interesting men teachers who can inspire and lead them to good lives instead of bad.

God depends on us—each one of us, not all of us at once.

When Jesus called his disciples, he made each one feel as if much depended on him. Of the twelve only Judas failed. The other eleven were faithful to death.

Today, nearly two thousand years later, Jesus depends on us as he did on his twelve.

What is your job as a Christian? What is mine? With God's help we must each decide for ourselves.

But never forget—you are important. Just one person, but still one. A very wise man said, "I am just one person, but I am one. I cannot do everything, but I can do something. And what I can do, I will do."

23. How Not to Be Defeated by a Horsefly

"Do not be overcome by evil, but overcome evil with good."—Rom. 12:21

MANY YEARS AGO WHEN I WAS A BOY, ONE OF MY BEST FRIENDS had four legs. No, he was not a dog but a horse.

Old Bob, as we called him, was our family horse. He was a horse of many parts. We rode him to the swimming hole, two, three, and sometimes four boys perched on his back. He pulled the wooden sled built especially for him.

And he pulled the plows and harrows that we used to break and cultivate the ground. He and I plowed many, many rows of corn, potatoes, beans, and almost every other vegetable you can mention. We spent a great many months together, old Bob and I.

One thing that annoyed me very much was the horsefly. And if this pesky creature annoyed me, how much more did it annoy old Bob! For horseflies are more apt to light on horses than human beings, naturally.

I could fight them off with my hands, but poor Bob was hitched to the plow and had little chance at these vicious insects, as large as the end of your thumb and with a terrible bite. They would often leave a spot of blood where they had bitten my friend.

Naturally I would stop plowing and try to kill the horseflies. Any decent master would.

But I soon found that if I tried to kill every horsefly that came along, no plowing got done. Sometimes I could switch at them with the cotton plowline as we went along the rows.

So despite my pity for my friend Bob I found it necessary to plow right along despite the flies, stopping now and then when one was just right for swatting and letting him have it. But if I waited until all the flies were gone, then no plowing was done.

You will discover in your life that when you try to do some worth-while task, you'll never lack for annoyances. There will always be people who'll say, "He can't do it!" or, "Why bother?" Every great leader has had his share of human horseflies who didn't help but simply got in the way.

Some individuals pay more attention to the irritations, hindrances, and hardships of life than they do to their own ideals, aims, and dreams. They fight little petty fights and stop to feud with people instead of pursuing their goals. Suppose big-league ball players began to talk back to every loud-mouthed razzer in the stands? But they don't. Their job is to play ball, not argue with the grandstands.

Someday you may be involved in a great project. If so, know what you must do, plan for it, and do it. Don't be distracted by anybody who wants to criticize but not help.

It is not easy to remain silent or keep right on when you feel irritated to the point of striking back. Not easy but essential.

I found this out by trying to ignore the horseflies—that old Bob and I got each job done and swatted quite a few of the little beasts on the way. But we never stopped work just to fight them.

24. You Can Begin Again

> *"Wash yourselves; make yourselves clean;*
> *remove the evil of your doings*
> *from before my eyes;*
> *cease to do evil,*
> *learn to do good."*
>
> —Isa. 1:16-17

DR. KELLER B. BRELAND OF HOT SPRINGS, ARKANSAS, IS ONE OF America's leading animal psychologists and experts on animal behavior. Believe it or not, he has trained chickens to play baseball and walk a tightrope. He trains raccoons to play basketball and a cow to ring a tiny school bell. Under his careful teaching hens learn to play "Yankee Doodle" without missing a note, a feat many boys and girls can't perform even after a year's piano lessons.

At Dr. Breland's farm near Hot Springs his "pupils" are given training they never forget.

That's just the point. They can't forget. They can't do their tricks wrong. Given the proper rewards, always a tidbit of their favorite food, they go through their motions machinelike with no notion of what they're doing. Dr. Breland says that these animals will always obey when given the right command or signal. No matter what the conditions, how noisy curious crowds might get, or whether they're on television or not, they go through their tricks.

All of which demonstrates how marvelously God made us and how different from animals. For we can change.

Not only does our heavenly Father let us perform badly if we desire, but with his help we can suddenly redirect our lives and become different and better people. We can change from stingy to generous. From bitter to sweet. From lazy to helpful. From lawless to obedient.

Unlike the animals, doomed to perform according to their master's commands, man can change at will. We are God's children. He gave only to man the power to become better.

Limitless opportunities for beginning again confront us every day. Can this particular task I am doing right this minute be done better than yesterday? What did I learn from the game I played yesterday? What were my mistakes and weak points? How can I improve?

What are my selfish and mean habits? Why not drop them and switch with God's assistance to new and better ways?

What about those wrongs, which we call sins, that we did yesterday, and last week, and last year? Have we told God we're sorry, asked his forgiveness, and resolved not to commit them again?

We can begin again. It's never too late. Remember the thief who was crucified beside Jesus Christ? In his dying hours he asked our Lord to save him. Jesus assured him that they would be together in paradise that very day! What wonderful news for a desperate man who saw his whole life ending in failure!

Not only does God tell us we can change; he gives us strength to change, to turn from wrong ways to right ones, to give ourselves to him instead of living selfishly. Jesus told us to pray in the Lord's Prayer, "Give us this day our daily bread." This means not only our three meals a day but also spiritual strength.

If you're not satisfied with your life, your situation is not hopeless by any means. If you want to change, you can with God's help.

Why be like one of Dr. Breland's animals or any animal, for that matter? Be a true child of God. You can begin again if you ask his help.

25. Are You Afraid to Fall Down?

(A Midwinter Question)

> *"Fear not, for I am with you,*
> *. . . for I am your God;*
> *I will strengthen you, I will help you."*
> —Isa. 41:10

PERHAPS YOU'RE ONE OF THOSE LEARNING TO ICE SKATE THIS winter—or ski.

What's the most difficult part of learning to skate or ski? It isn't getting the right position for your ankles, or putting your knees thus and so, or tightening the straps. Nor is the actual physical pain very great when you take a tumble.

The hardest part of learning these sports for most boys and girls is this—overcoming the fear of falling. And what's so bad about falling, especially at your age?

You know perfectly well that you've fallen a hundred times without being more than slightly bruised. You can take tumbles all day long without winding up in the hospital or doctor's office.

It isn't the bumps or bruises or aching shins we dread the

most, is it? No, what we fear more than the physical pain is *being laughed at*. This hurts most of all.

And who laughs loudest when beginners take a tumble? Is it the best skaters? No, quite often it's those who can't skate well themselves.

How silly that other people's laughter should keep us from doing what we want to do and what we really should do. But it happens all the time. And to grownups as well as children.

Davy Crockett said, "Be sure you are right, then go ahead."

If in your heart you want to achieve something badly and that something is right and proper for you, expect a few laughs from the sidelines. For that's where they usually come from. From the grandstands where others sit and watch but don't have the courage to try themselves.

History is full of examples of great men being laughed at. Dr. Charles Kettering was told he couldn't build a self-starter for the automobile. It would have to be as big as the car motor, they said. Many years ago automobiles were cranked by hand— that is, you got out in front of your car and turned the motor over by hand. That was about the time Charles Kettering did the "impossible" and invented the automatic electric starter. Kettering wasn't afraid to fail—to fall short of his aim. Thus he succeeded by his very daring.

The world has always been populated with the scorners, the laughers who poke fun at the achievers, the unskilled who take out their own failures by pointing fingers at those who try.

I wish I could guarantee your being a good skater and skier without falling. A few very good athletes can do this. Most of us have to fall and get up, fall and get up, and repeat this routine until we've trained our muscles properly.

All your life you'll discover that it isn't the falling that hurts but the fear of being thought ridiculous. As you grow older, you will have far more difficult challenges than learning to skate.

If you can conquer now your fear of being laughed at, you can meet these challenges twice as easily than if you listen for sideline snickers. Pray to God. Ask him to give you courage. In the Bible we read:

> Fear not, for I am with you,
>
> . . . .
>
> I will strengthen you, I will help you.

With God helping you, the falls, tumbles, and even people's laughter can be taken without really hurting.

26. The Unknown Man on a Winning Team

"Let us have no self-conceit, no provoking of one another, no envy of one another."—Gal. 5:26

EACH YEAR AT WORLD SERIES TIME SPORTS PAGES CARRY TWO very interesting pictures, at least interesting to me. These are the group photographs of the two pennant-winning teams.

There they sit, row upon row—players, manager, coaches, and bat boy. Usually not in the picture but very important are the scouts who look for new talent and who spy on opposing teams. Also not shown are the office workers and those who work on the business side of the game.

About forty men usually get in the picture, and although they are considered important enough to be shown, how very few of their names can even a sports-minded reader be sure of. But all of these unfamiliar faces and names are important— in their way just as important as the heavy hitters and good pitchers who make the headlines. Their salaries are lower, their names are not in the papers so much, but without them there couldn't be a team.

Multiply forty by sixteen, the number of big-league teams,

and you have over six hundred almost unknown big-league ball players. Then count up the hundreds and hundreds of other minor-league players playing on the "farm" teams of the majors and you realize what a vast number it takes to produce a pennant race and finally the big event we call the World Series.

Are these unknown players envious or jealous of the few big stars who get the top money and front pages? Perhaps some are, but the majority probably aren't. And anyway, for better or worse, they are essential to big-league ball playing.

Life is like baseball in this respect. Every city, factory, church, and any kind of organization requires a vast majority of people who never acquire fame—yet they're as important as those who do.

Just in the Church alone many, many men and women work year after year without any praise, or pay, or recognition. They teach Sunday school; they help clean up the building; they help raise money; they visit homes of new people in town; they help with suppers; they read their Bibles and pray at home for others. They never preach from the pulpit, but without them there could be no church.

Most homes contain a mother who stays in the background. She works from early morning to late at night for her husband and children. She sends them out dressed well and clean. She listens to their troubles. She encourages them. These mothers whom we take for granted make our homes good ones.

If you're in any group, on any team, in any school class activity, remember the big-league ball players and how few of them reap the glory of headlines and big pay. Do your best. If you're one of the stars, fine. If you're not, play on the team the best you can.

Jesus had twelve leading disciples. We know the names of these twelve and a few other followers, but just a few. What valiant souls and stalwart heroes there must have been among the unknown many! They helped make the Christian Church too.

Who was the Unknown Soldier? Nobody knows. His body lies at Arlington, Virginia. He symbolizes those unknown thousands of soldiers who gave their lives for America.

Give your best, whether a star or just one of the many. Your reward will come in time.

27. A Minister Who Invented Basketball

"And whatever you do, in word or deed, do everything in the name of the Lord Jesus, giving thanks to God the Father through him."—Col. 3:17

WHAT IS AMERICA'S MOST POPULAR SPORT?

Baseball? Wrong. Baseball is called our national pastime, but it is not our most popular sport. Basketball is.

It is perhaps the youngest of all our athletic games, being invented by a single man in December, 1891. I shall tell the story of this man, for I think it is important that he be regarded just as much a Christian hero as any great preacher or missionary or doctor. Any person who can bring to the world the good that basketball has brought and in such a fine, wholesome way deserves attention.

James Naismith was a Presbyterian minister. He was very highly educated with eleven college degrees, one of them in music. He was born and raised on a farm in Ontario, Canada, where he did much very hard work driving teams, chopping wood, sawing logs, walking, hunting, fishing, and the many other chores and sports a farm boy of that period enjoyed.

He entered McGill University in Montreal, planning to be a minister. When he graduated from McGill in 1887, he was the best gymnastic athlete of his class. Upon graduation he became athletic director for the university, getting paid enough to continue his studies at the Presbyterian Theological Seminary, where he studied to become a minister.

Then he thought that he would be a different kind of minister—one who taught Christian living through sports. So he came to the United States and entered the Y.M.C.A. School in Springfield, Massachusetts.

There young Naismith was impressed by the lack of any winter sport that would be played in between the football and baseball seasons.

Instead of accepting the situation, which others had done, Naismith got busy. Adapting an old game he once played back at home, he obtained two round bushel peach baskets, mounted them on poles ten feet high, divided the students into two teams of nine men each, tossed them a soccer ball—and the great game of basketball was thus invented!

The game took awhile to develop with the present rules. Actually an old drawing shows a janitor standing at the top of a ladder to pick the ball from out of the peach basket whenever a goal was made. A pretty dangerous job.

For some time also any number of players was allowed. At Cornell University, where the game became an instant hit, over a hundred students were on the court at once. Imagine trying to referee a basketball game with fifty players on each side! Finally in 1895 the rule of a five-man team was drawn up.

Although Naismith never became the pastor of a church, he had a wide Christian influence. He read and reread his Bible. He marked it up, underlining the verses that meant most to him. He was a Christian gentleman in every way, teaching others and living in his own life the ideals of Jesus Christ.

His main interest was never in basketball itself but in the Christian life of those who played it. How they played and how they lived were far more important to him than the number of points they made.

When James Naismith, the Presbyterian minister, died on November 28, 1939, after forty years as head of the athletic department at the University of Kansas, not many Americans knew much about him. The game he invented over fifty years ago was far better known than the inventor, and is so today.

For of the 150,000,000 people in America who pay to see basketball games every year, certainly very few know anything about the man James Naismith. But his influence they know. They know that basketball is not only our most popular game but one of our finest, helping to build strong bodies, clean sportsmanship, and fine characters. What the man did is far better known than the man himself. But the world is a better place because of James Naismith, the farm boy from Ontario, Canada.

We can learn much from Naismith's life. All of us have chances to help the world. Few of us will be long remembered. But endless opportunities lie all around just the same. And whether people give us credit or not isn't the point. God knows what we do. No sincere effort goes unnoticed by him. He knows and he cares.

Let's each give to the world what we can. The number of people who know or care isn't important. What is important is that we use our minds, bodies, and talents to make them richer, not poorer.

28. Big Leaguer Jackie Robinson

"And Peter . . . said: 'Truly, I perceive that God shows no partiality, but in every nation any one who fears him and does what is right is acceptable to him."

—Acts 10:34-35

TAKE YOUR MIND BACK TO MAY, 1920, TO A HOT DAY IN GEORGIA. Mallie Robinson was discouraged. And no wonder! Her husband had run away and left her with five children to raise, the oldest only ten.

She hitched up the horse and went out in the fields to plow under the broiling afternoon sun. Furrow after furrow, row after row, step after weary step, she plowed until the day was done and she returned to the house. There in the half darkness inside was her baby—John Roosevelt Robinson.

This sixteen-month-old Negro boy, who cried constantly, whose mother was soon to board a bus with just the clothes on her back and five hungry tots, was the same Jackie Robinson who someday was to be on the front page and sports page of every newspaper in the world.

The bus roared on toward California, the Robinsons eating mainly sandwiches and lunches brought along, for Negroes could not be served at most of the bus stops along the way.

We've no time to tell each incident in the life of this great ball player who, as much as anybody else, brought the Brooklyn Dodgers to their first World Series victory, but let's just take a quick glimpse at him along the way.

First, his grandfather was a slave. His mother, when they reached California, took in washing and ironing to feed her family. Oftentimes she worked out in other folks's houses. After school and in the summer Jackie went around the streets of Pasadena gathering up newspapers and junk in a little red wagon. He shined shoes for more money for the family. Each Sunday morning he got up at four to deliver newspapers.

When the great depression of 1929 came, times were hard. Some nights there was no supper. Jackie and the other four children knew hunger. But they were happy.

And no matter what, every Sunday morning they all walked to the Methodist church nearby, where Jackie learned Christian ideals that are with him to this day. Mallie Robinson always reminded her children, no matter how poor they were to worship God and give him thanks.

But harder than poverty was being called a "nigger" and having to take it. Jackie was hot-tempered. He wanted to strike back. But his mother showed him how he could win only if he was more charitable and patient than those who called him names.

Jackie and his older brother Matthew soon acquired fame as athletes. Matthew even came in second in the 1936 Olympics, right behind the great Jesse Owens in the two hundred meter sprint.

Jackie was an all-round athlete. In Muir Technical High School he entered every sport, starring in track, baseball, basketball, and football. But in them all the worst opponent was never the actual competition but the cruel talk and foul play he encountered because of his color.

We see him being tackled harder than the other backs in football, or being guarded more closely on the basketball court, or the fans calling him bad names from the baseball stands. Jackie learned that if he was to stay in the game, he had to keep his mouth shut.

He matured and gained fame at Pasadena Junior College and then at the University of California at Los Angeles. He graduated from there as the greatest athlete in the school's history.

Even while in college with this great athletic career Jackie had to work—cleaning up dirty dishes in a cafeteria, working as janitor, selling hot dogs and candy at Rose Bowl games, which are held in Pasadena, his home town.

The years passed. Jackie was called into the army in World War II. Then he coached sports at a small, struggling Negro college in Houston, Texas. Next he played for the Kansas City baseball club in a minor league.

Then came his big chance. Branch Rickey, manager of the Brooklyn Dodgers, asked him to play for Montreal as preparation for actually going on to the Dodgers. Rickey warned him against the jeers, curses, blows, intentional spikings, and vile names he'd

69

have to endure and all without striking back or lashing out with his tongue.

All of what Rickey said came true. Not only the fans but the players did all they could to get under Jackie's skin. Every bad word was hurled at him. Players deliberately roughed him up to make him lose his temper and be thrown out of the game. But Jackie Robinson, the first Negro in big-league baseball, held his tongue and his fist.

We know now how he did make the Dodger team and in his first year was named the most valuable rookie of the year. Honor after honor was heaped on him by Negro and white person alike. When he tried to buy a home in Stamford, Connecticut, neighbors opposed it, saying they didn't want Negroes living so close. But others said differently. And Jackie and his wife got the home they wanted.

Through all these trials his Christian religion, taught so many years ago by his mother, stayed by him. He learned to smile when mistreated, to play all the harder when opponents tried to rattle him.

Today the whole world honors Jackie Robinson, the Christian gentleman, the same Jackie born many years ago in a tumble-down house, but who had the advantage of having a mother who followed Christ.

29. Toyohiko Kagawa— The Japanese Christian Hero

"And I tell you, everyone who acknowledges me before men, the Son of man also will acknowledge before the angels of God."—Luke 12:8

SINCE GOD MADE THE VARIOUS COLORS OF HUMAN SKIN—WHITE, yellow, red, and brown—it is only natural that he would love all people of all colors. God hates nobody. He loves everybody. People with yellow skins come mainly from three countries— China, Korea, and Japan. China alone has over 650,000,000 persons. One person out of four on the earth is a Chinese.

Very few out of all the millions of yellow men, women, boys, and girls in Asia are actually Christian, for only comparatively recently have our Christian missionaries gone there to tell of Christ. But those few Christians who are there have great influence for their numbers. Many of them become Christian at the risk of their lives, giving up even the love of their families, who tell them they are forsaking their old family gods.

One such brave person, a truly great Christian hero, is Toyohiko Kagawa, born in 1888. His parents were people of wealth. He had a great future as a brilliant young man.

But something, or rather somebody, upset his life of comfort, ease, and luxury. That somebody was Jesus Christ. Kagawa heard of Christ, the Son of God, who came to earth, suffered, and died for us and for him, Toyohiko Kagawa. Such a great love impressed the young Kagawa. Here was the answer to great questions that had been in his mind.

Furthermore, he was terribly troubled by the slums in his country. How could he sleep nights when human beings lived under such conditions? Whole families in one room without windows. Small children working long hours.

The young Kagawa had compassion on the slum dwellers, even as his Master, Jesus Christ, had compassion on the multitudes nearly two thousand years ago.

When he announced that he was going to move into a small room in the slums and help all who came his way, his family said No. Furthermore, they opposed his becoming a Christian.

Just how Kagawa stood firmly against his parents' opposition, how he rented a room and gradually built up a settlement house in the slums, how he organized workingmen's clubs to buy their food cheaper, how he organized workers to secure better

71

pay—all these are just a few of the thrilling achievements in one man's life.

He caught a dreaded eye disease in the slums. He was never strong physically, and when I heard him speak here in America once, I was impressed with his smallness and frailty. I wondered, How can such a small and weak-looking man do so much for God?

But when he began to speak, I knew the answer. For here was a man dedicated completely to Christ and to God. He has not the slightest selfishness to hinder his working for others. Furthermore, he likes to laugh and make others laugh.

During World War II Kagawa spent years in jail for opposing the Japanese military policy which oppressed helpless people and that finally brought the United States into the war and defeated the Japanese. Kagawa pointed out how war settles nothing and how his whole nation would suffer because of its cruel acts.

After the war he was released immediately and was one of the greatest forces in bringing friendship back between America and Japan. He came to America and was warmly greeted wherever he went.

To look at Kagawa one cannot help but wonder: How can such a tiny, weak-looking little man do so much?

The answer is: God can use any of us to do his will if we but let him. This little yellow-skinned man, Toyohiko Kagawa, the most loved man in Japan, is proof of that.

30. A Little Brown Man Who Freed His Nation

"Love your enemies and pray for those who persecute you."
—Matt. 5:44

WHEN WE THINK OF PATRIOTS WHO FREE THEIR LANDS FROM foreign oppressors, we usually have in mind daring military geniuses who lead poorly clad and ill-equipped armies against superior outside forces and finally drive the enemy off their lands.

Most liberators of the world have done just this.

But the man who freed the second largest nation in the world from foreign rule never fired a shot. He never used a rifle or fired a cannon. In fact, he forbade his followers from using any kind of force against their enemies.

Mohandas K. Gandhi was a funny-looking little brown man, a citizen of India. He owned no property except his spectacles, his Bible, and a few other personal articles.

As a young man he acquired a high education, attending Oxford University in England. Once while in South Africa he saw the terrible injustice of race prejudice when he was ordered one night to leave a train compartment reserved for white people. When he refused to leave, he was pushed off the train at the next station.

He took the stagecoach. He was called vile names and beaten. No hotel would give him a room.

Then and there Gandhi dedicated himself to a peaceful, steady campaign of liberation of his people, and without using force or violence.

When he returned to his native India, he began a program of education using the teachings of Christ. Although not a Christian but a Hindu, he recognized Christ's greatness. He saw that as Christ had rejected force and killing as methods of winning victory, so he, Gandhi, would too.

The British at that time controlled and ruled India. With love in his heart for the British, Gandhi showed the Indians how they must disobey oppressive laws. Soon the jails were filled with Indians. Two of them were Gandhi and a young man named Nehru, later to be India's prime minister.

Soldiers beat the Indians, clubbed them with rifles, and

abused them in all sorts of brutal ways. Still the Indians refused to strike the British.

During World War II when the British had to fight the Japanese, Gandhi called off his independence campaign so that he would not be taking unfair advantage. After the war, though, he started up again.

By this time the British, so impressed by Gandhi's character and knowing that they could not keep over 300,000,000 Indians under their rule, decided to give India freedom.

The most amazing fact about this new freedom was that India decided to remain friendly with England and, instead of cutting off all ties, became a member of the British Commonwealth of Nations, a world-wide group of independent countries bound by loyalty to certain democratic ideals originating in England.

Thus Gandhi won two major victories without firing a shot—his nation gained complete independence, and he made a friend of a former enemy country.

Today the whole world honors this tiny brown man who refused to hate or kill. In 1948 he was killed by a fanatic, but even those who opposed him wept at hearing of his death.

Doesn't the world need more men like Mohandas Gandhi today?

31. What Will You Be When You Grow Up?

"Do your best to present yourself to God as one approved, a workman who has no need to be ashamed."
—II Tim. 2:15

WHAT BOY OR GIRL HASN'T DAYDREAMED ABOUT THIS QUESTION? What boy hasn't seen himself exploring some faraway ocean

74

island, or zooming out into the sky in a spaceship, or leading a crew of men into unexplored territory?

What girl hasn't thought of herself years hence with a good job, or with a nice husband and several children, running her home as she thinks a home should be run?

There's nothing wrong with daydreaming about your future. As a matter of fact, there's something wrong when we don't. For out of dreams come real life. Only if we just dream and then dream some more without any kind of action is there harm. First must come dreams, wishes, thoughts, and plans—then a way of making all these come true.

What will you be when you grow up? More than you think, you will be what your dreams, plans, and hard work determine.

Just as important as your dreams, however, is the way you are living now, for these days of girlhood and boyhood are the foundation stones for tomorrow, next week, next month, next year, and the years to follow.

The kind of body you are building through exercise and work will have much to do with what kind of body you will have when grown up—weak, strong or just average. Are you building a rugged, strong, healthy body? It can't be done while slouched down in an easy chair watching television programs.

What kind of mind are you building? Are you doing your schoolwork in school and at home as perfectly as you can each day, not quitting until your papers are neat, correct, and the best you can do? Believe it or not, the kind of job you do thirty years from now will be done in much the same manner you do your homework. For the habits we form as children are frequently the habits of later years too.

What kind of soul are you shaping now? Do you always think of yourself first, getting what you can for yourself first and letting others wait? Do you try to make peace instead of argument? Do you criticize others or help them? Do you think the world is mean to you, or do you look for ways to make the world a better place to live in? What kind of soul, or spirit, do you have now? The answer to this will tell you much about what kind of person you'll be ten, twenty, and thirty years from now.

God gives to his children the longest growing period of any of his creatures. We need all these years of childhood and youth to build lives that can be called great. Fine men and women do not just happen but come from many years of hard preparation.

Now in these years God gives you is the time to become the kind of man or woman you want to be. Each day is like a brick or stone placed in the house of your life. Is it well placed? Will it make your house stronger and more beautiful?

Use these years well. That is why God gives us so many, to become the kind of persons he wants us to be.

32. Invisible Things Are the Strongest

"God is love."—I John 4:8

THE MAGNET I HOLD IN MY HAND IS NOTHING NEW OR STRANGE. See how it pulls this nail or this tack. See how the iron filings on this sheet of paper are instantly arranged in lines when you put the magnet directly under the paper.

We have all seen a magnet at work, yet mysteriously enough we don't know how it works. We even harness the force of magnetism to lift huge piles of scrap iron. Every big junk yard has one of those big magnetic cranes. Turn on the electricity and the crane magnet picks up hundreds of pounds of iron. Turn it off and the iron drops.

The earth and moon are both magnets, attracting each other enough so they won't fly apart. And in turn, the sun is a huge magnet holding the earth so it won't fly into space. It does the same for the other planets too—Mars, Venus, Neptune, Mercury, and the rest.

Going farther away is the Milky Way, that vast, flat disk of hundreds of millions of stars. What holds them together in one star system? Magnetism. Invisible magnetism.

Magnetism is the name for the force, or strength, that we can't see but that makes one piece of matter draw closer to another. No human being has ever seen magnetism, or taken a picture of it, or felt it rush past his face while running, as you can feel air. Yet its force is tremendous. Enough to keep our earth and sun from flying apart.

Like many other forces of nature, magnetism does its work with absolutely no sound. Nobody has ever heard it, no matter how much they listened. Nor smelled or touched it.

The strongest forces on earth are not those which make the biggest bang. No, the strongest are generally the quietest. And the strongest force of all is the love of God. It is invisible, untouchable, and has never been seen by the eye of man.

But like magnetism its effect can be felt. Through Jesus Christ, God showed us how much he loves us. And people all around who live by God's ways display in a quiet manner that love is stronger than evil.

By his love God draws us to him as our parents' love draws us to them. Stronger than even magnetism, the love of God unites us with him.

33. How Dirty-Looking Bread Mold
May Save Your Life

> *"The stone which the builders rejected*
> *has become the chief cornerstone."*
> —Ps. 118:22

HERE IN MY HAND I HOLD A PERFECTLY GOOD PIECE OF BREAD
that none of you would eat. Why? Because of the dirty-looking
blackish-grey mold on it.

You might think it's poisonous, but it isn't. The bread just
looks unfit to eat. Actually it won't hurt you, for I've eaten many
a piece of bread worse looking than this.

But God's ways are different from ours. Just how different
and how much better were revealed when Dr. Mario Stefanini
of St. Elizabeth's Hospital in Boston discovered an amazing
truth about this bread mold that causes so many people to
throw moldly bread away.

Dr. Stefanini discovered through research that this very mold,
if injected into the human blood stream, has the power to dissolve blood clots anywhere in the body within a matter of a few
minutes.

What a wonderful discovery! For every day all over America
and all over the world people are dying because blood clots form
at such vital places as the heart or brain.

And now we learn that this mold that disgusts so many by its
appearance may save our lives. Blood clots that shut off the flow
of blood to various parts of our bodies are extremely dangerous.
Sometimes they cause instant death. Other times they cause
long, serious illnesses, especially in older people.

But Dr. Stefanini tells us that lives once given up can be
saved—and by the injection of a mold that mankind has regarded as an enemy for thousands of years.

The Bible tells us: Let nothing that God has created be
called common or unclean.

God has created everything with a purpose in mind. Every
single plant and animal of the many, many thousands of kinds

are put on earth for some reason. Who would have ever thought of bread mold as medicine? But now it is, a most precious kind of medicine.

Sometimes we look down on God's creatures that appear unattractive. They are products of God's mind, just the same as you and I. The jellyfish in the sea, the weeds in the garden, the grass by the roadside, the eagle atop the cliff—all these and the thousands and thousands of other forms of life are part of God's wonderful creation.

Perhaps you think of certain men and women or boys and girls as not being created and loved by God. If so, how mistaken you are.

For every person has a purpose. God can use us all to help him. No matter how unattractive we are, this still remains true.

If God can create an ugly bread mold with the power to stop blood clots and save lives, can he not have great purposes for us also?

34. Don't Be Afraid to Ask Questions

" 'What have I done now?' said David [to his brothers]; 'I merely asked a question.' "—I Sam. 17:29 (Moffatt)

An old poem goes:

> I have six honest serving men.
> They taught me all I know.
> Their names are What and Where and When
> And Why and How and Who.

ONE GOOD SIGN OF INTELLIGENCE IS ASKING QUESTIONS. NOT EM-barrassing questions, such as little brother or sister might ask in front of company, but just curious questions.

79

A six-year-old girl asked such an embarrassing question. When a friend of her mother's arrived at the front door, the girl asked: "How long is she going to stay?" Actually she was just asking the question that was in her mind.

As far as we know, animals do not question. They simply accept the world and the universe as they find it. Likely no snake or squirrel or monkey ever gazed at the moon and asked itself: How far is it away? or, Is it really made of green cheese?

Human beings were meant to ask questions. Take away this power and we become less than human.

The Bible is full of great questions. David, the shepherd boy, bringing his older brothers rations, asked them concerning the giant Goliath, "Why doesn't somebody do something to this pagan who insults the Lord God?" When they reprimanded their kid brother for this remark, he said, "All I did was ask a question." His question led him to King Saul and eventually to Israel's throne.

One man came to Jesus with a burning question: "What must I do to be saved?"

The only mention of Jesus as a boy that we find in all four Gospels was the scene in the Temple. His parents found him, twelve years old, asking the learned teachers there questions they couldn't answer. Perhaps he asked them *Why* and *What* and *When*.

James Isaac Newton, the great English scientist who is ranked along with Albert Einstein, was sitting in his garden one day. An apple fell *thump!* to the ground. He asked himself: Why does an apple fall *down?* Why doesn't it fall *up?* Why, why, why? Out of these questions in the garden came our ideas about gravity and attraction of physical bodies.

All our great scientific advances have come from questions and answers to these questions.

Also all our great advances in medicine, law, politics, and religion came because somebody dared to ask questions. Many men have died because they asked embarrassing questions of unjust rulers.

Every thinking person should ask questions, too, about themselves. These questions are the greatest and most important of all. Such as:

Why am I? What am I here for? What does God want me to do? How will I make a living? Where should I live? Whom should I marry?

If you are like most boys and girls, you want to know the answer to these badly. How you answer them will determine what kind of person you'll be.

The Bible gives us the great answers to our questions. Jesus especially gives us the best ones. Read the answers he gave to questioners he faced, and you'll find your own answers there in print.

Keep asking questions. Never stop. And someday you'll find the answers you want. For Jesus said, "Ask, and it will be given."

35. Science—Man's Peephole into God's Workshop

"The heavens are telling the glory of God;
and the firmament proclaims his handiwork"
—Ps. 19:1

IN MY HAND I HOLD A LARGE PIECE OF CARDBOARD. HOLDING IT BEfore my face, I can see almost nothing before me. This piece of cardboard we'll call ignorance.

In the center of this cardboard is a tiny hole made with a pin. Let's call this hole *science*.

Take a peek through this peephole and you can see just a

few objects on the other side. What you can see compares with what one man can see and understand about nature.

In real life man creates a peephole with his mind—his God-given intelligence. We are so curious about nature we put our eyes up to this peephole and try to peer through.

We use various instruments for this purpose—telescopes, microscopes, all kinds of measuring and weighing instruments, and those intricate machines and delicate instruments used by scientists today. Sometimes we look and look and say that nature is like this or that. And everybody agrees.

For thousands of years men looked at the sun as it seemed to move overhead and concluded: The sun travels round the earth. Then we took another look and thought another thought and concluded: No, the earth moves round the sun.

Scientists are continually taking another look, always open-minded to the suspicion that if they saw more, their old ideas might change.

It was less than one hundred years ago that men discovered through the peephole of the microscope how many diseases are caused by tiny living organisms we call "germs."

So vast and complicated and marvelous is God's world of nature that no single person can learn and remember much of the total. And the more we learn of some branch of knowledge, the more we see yet undiscovered. Some people have worried lest we may someday learn as much as God knows.

How ridiculous and childish! How utterly impossible!

Nobody knows better how silly this is than do our smartest scientists.

The ancient psalmist King David felt so impressed and overpowered by God's creations that he wrote: "The heavens are telling the glory of God." David also wrote:

> In his hand are the depths of the earth;
> the heights of the mountains are his also.

The sea is his, for he made it;
for his hands formed the dry land.

God creates nature for men to learn about, to use, to take care of, to enjoy. To understand and appreciate nature, our Father has given us curiosity to make us ask questions and intelligence to provide the answers.

Every new discovery made by looking through the peephole of science only shows us how wonderful, powerful, and perfect is God.

And how it must please him for us to learn more of his works!

36. God's Guideline on the Highway of Life

"Blessed are those whose way is blameless,
who walk in the law of the Lord."

—Ps. 119:1

HIGHWAY ENGINEERS SAY THAT PERHAPS THE GREATEST SINGLE life-saving device ever invented for use on the road, other than a careful driver, is the white line down the middle.

You have seen this line and the signs along the road that say "Don't cross solid line on your side."

We have them in every state. When the line is dotted, that means go ahead and pass a car if another isn't coming. When there are two solid lines, with a yellow one on your side, that means "Danger. Don't pass." These danger points are usually on curves and on hilltops. Foolish drivers who disregard these signs endanger themselves and innocent people.

For they are put there for a purpose. The engineers who designed the roads know just where you can pass safely and where you cannot. They know from experience and study. Their whole lives are devoted to building roads.

God, the builder of the road of life, has put similar signs on that highway to warn us of danger spots. Mankind has found from thousands of years of experience that certain areas should have certain rules and laws. God has provided these rules, given to us through men like Moses and even more through his Son Jesus Christ.

For example, through Moses he gave us the Ten Commandments. If we disregard these commandments, we hurt ourselves and others.

What are these road signs of life? Here are the main ten as we find them in the Old Testament:

1. Thou shalt have no other gods before me.
2. Thou shalt not make unto thee any graven image.
3. Thou shalt not take the name of the Lord thy God in vain.
4. Remember the sabbath day, to keep it holy.
5. Honour thy father and thy mother.
6. Thou shalt not kill.
7. Thou shalt not commit adultery.
8. Thou shalt not steal.
9. Thou shalt not bear false witness against thy neighbour.
10. Thou shalt not covet.

Jesus gave us other road signs of life. And if we don't obey these also, we bring disaster on ourselves. Some of his main guiding sayings are:

"Thou shalt love the Lord thy God with all thy heart, and with all thy soul, and with all thy mind. . . . Thou shalt love thy neighbour as thyself."

"A new commandment I give unto you, That ye love one another; as I have loved you."

He gave us other signs for the road of life, too many to mention here, but if we obey these, we shall live truly God-like lives.

God knows all the road of life. He knows far better than we the danger points. He knows our weaknesses. And he loves us so much he is pained when we disobey his warnings and bring grief to ourselves and his other children.

Traveling the highways or traveling the road of life, we have plenty of markers for safe going—if we only obey the signs!

37. What Does It Cost to Be a Christian?

"Blessed are you when men revile you and persecute you and utter all kinds of evil against you falsely on my account."

—Matt. 5:11

"WHY IT COSTS NOTHING," SOME WOULD REPLY. BUT HOW MIS-taken they would be.

Being a follower of Jesus Christ is very expensive. If not, then we don't follow him very closely.

True, God gave his Son to the world. And Jesus Christ gave his life to save us from sin and death. He did this gladly, so great was his love for you and me.

But never be deceived. Anything fine and great can be achieved only at great cost.

For example, when we say we want to be Christians, or followers and imitators of Christ, we must first give up these things:

1. Selfishness.

2. Bad habits which we like but which are against God's will.

3. Putting our interests ahead of God's.

Now these are just three costs. We could list many more.

Perhaps the greatest cost is to be so grateful for God's gift of his Son that we feel sinful before him and ask his forgiveness for our sins. Then we must ask God to help us be Christians. Many people are too proud to do this. They think they can run their lives without God. They are wrong.

Then, being a Christian should cost us money. If you are a stingy, ungenerous Christian, then this won't be so. Many boys and girls, for example, spend from twenty-five cents to a dollar a week on themselves and take a nickel to church. But God isn't fooled.

Some grownups are very stingy Christians too. They give a dollar to the church but gladly spend many dollars on their own fun and pleasure.

Just what kind of Christian does this? A stingy Christian.

Once a rich young man came to Jesus asking what he could do to have everlasting life in heaven. Jesus saw how much he loved his money so he said: "Sell what you have, and give to the poor." The cost was too great. The young man went away sad, for he simply couldn't do that.

Being a Christian costs much in time also. Some church members don't like to have Christ interfere with their plans and convenience. They will attend church at Easter and Christmas and occasionally in between. Not wanting to spend their time worshiping God, they have a cheap religion. Naturally, the church doesn't fail, for there are always generous Christians who will give time teaching Sunday school and doing the many other extras that the church needs.

Jesus talked as much about money as he did any other topic. How he disliked cheap, stingy religion! He who was planning to give his whole life and finally die on the cruel cross was angered and saddened by those who gave of themselves and their money as little as possible.

When he died, Jesus left no money. But so great was his gift of his own life that millions of people since have eagerly made great sacrifices to carry on his way.

Is it wrong to give a nickel to church and spend a quarter for a soda?

Is it wrong to spend fifty cents for a movie and give a dime to church?

Is it wrong to watch TV ten hours a week and not have time to attend Sunday school and church two hours on Sunday?

You give your own answers to these questions.

Yes, the Christian religion costs much. It costs all we have.

Like anything in life great and fine and grand, it costs.

It costs time, effort, money, sacrifice, inconvenience.

But without great cost we really get nothing in this life truly worth while. Even while very young we know that what comes easily or cheaply means little to us. We hold dear those things we want badly enough to give our best. Let us thank God that Jesus Christ promises a life here and after death, too, that is worth all we can give.

38. Do Not Despise the Little Things

"Why, even the hairs of your head are all numbers."
—Luke 12:7

IN THIS GLASS JAR BEFORE ME IS COMMON, ORDINARY SOIL FROM my garden. If I should ask you, What's in it? you would correctly reply, "Why, just dirt!"

Garden dirt is right. But there's something else too.

If we could take a microscope and peer ever so closely at this dirt, we could see literally millions of tiny plants and animals wriggling and moving and shoving and crawling and eating one another. Some are shaped like a corkscrew, others are long like a pencil, some are fat like a toy balloon, while others are oval like a football.

We call them bacteria or microbes. And wherever there is soil where plants grow, you will find them, billions of them per square yard. You find them in ditches alongside the road, on your

87

hands, under your fingernails, in your hair, in your mouth, and yes, even inside you, in your tummy. Without them the bigger plants and animals couldn't live. They help digest our food. Some are harmful to human beings, but most are helpful. They curdle milk to help us manufacture cheese and butter. They make our bread rise. And when cultivated and purified correctly, they make up the wonder drugs that cause us to get over illnesses so quickly.

God created the tiny things as well as the big things and a great many more of them. Just consider our own bodies, for example. Inside us are over 60,000 miles of extremely small blood vessels we call capillaries, small tubes so tiny that only one blood cell at a time can squeeze through carrying life-giving oxygen and food and carrying away from the body cells waste products and carbon dioxide. Yes, inside us are enough capillaries, if stretched out, to go around this world and have some left over. Without them the big veins and arteries couldn't do their work.

Frequently you and I may feel that we are so small and unimportant in this world that we don't need to work for God. "How can he need us?" we ask ourselves.

And how wrong we are if we think this!

Once Jesus wanted to feed a huge crowd who came to hear him preach. They were hungry yet miles away from the nearest store. One of his disciples said: "Master, there is a lad here with five loaves and two fishes." From that lad's lunch Jesus created enough food to feed thousands.

No matter who you are or what you or others think of you or your family, God considers you important. What you have, what you are, and what you can give to the world are important. No, not just important but absolutely necessary.

We live in a strange age when we are impressed by bigness. But all big things depend on little things. And God's plan for each of us depends on the thousands and thousands of small acts, thoughts, and deeds we perform every day. Do not think what you do each moment is not important, for out of these moments, piled one on top of another into hours, days, weeks, months, and years, is your life built.

Do not make the mistake of despising the small things, for God made them and cares for them. Upon each of them and each of us he depends for his work to be done.

39. The Greatest Worker Makes the Least Noise

"In quietness and in trust shall be your strength."
—Isa. 30:15

DON'T WE USUALLY CONNECT LOUD NOISE WITH WORK?

What a racket our great machines make! Perhaps you've seen highways being built. Great earthmovers, concrete mixers, power shovels, and ditch diggers with their big diesel motors make a terrific rattle, clackety, clack, rumble, and groaning. And when rock is blasted to make way for the highway, what a big boom!

Or go in a busy factory. In some you can't hear yourself talk. Or stand by a busy street crossing when all the cars and trucks start up as the light turns green. The very earth shakes with the racket.

So we might easily believe that work and noise must always go together.

But the world's greatest worker does most of the world's work in complete silence or with very little noise. We are so busy listening to man-made noises we don't take time to think that all about us God is causing great changes right under our noses and with absolutely no sound whatever. Or with very little.

Consider the important ways his work is done. The grass

89

under our feet, in the cow pastures, on the prairies of the West and the plains of Europe, Asia, Africa, and South America—this grass that covers millions of square miles—is the food for all grazing animals. Without it we wouldn't have milk on the table. All this grass grows without a sound.

So do the other crops on which human life depends grow—tomatoes, potatoes, bananas, beans, squash, peaches, apples, and the hundreds of other crops that give us life.

God sends rain. It makes some noise but very little. Yet rain makes all things grow. He sends snow in the winter to melt and settle deep inside the earth and provide moisture in the dry months. How silently snow falls. You can barely hear it on even the stillest night!

Every day sunshine bathes the whole earth—yet with no sound. Without the sun human life would soon vanish.

The work our human minds perform—how silent that is! The brain sends signals to our muscles, telling them what to do or not to do. And without the faintest whisper of noise. God works through our brains.

The winds sweep around the earth, never stopping. They bring moisture from the ocean to the land. We hear the wind when it rushes through the treetops or around the eaves of the house, but otherwise it goes by silently, most of it high above our heads. The work done by the earth's winds is so great we can't possibly measure it.

And everywhere around us in plant and animal life of all sorts God silently goes about his business. The life processes with our own bodies, for example, are all done silently.

I could go on to list the silent works done by man, too, and show how most of our best work is done silently. But let's save that for another time.

So don't mistake noise for power or work. Don't mistake man's noise for God's voice. For he speaks and works quietly. And we should stop and listen more often.

40. Men with No Money Who Left Us Great Riches

"Do not lay up for yourselves treasures on earth, . . . but lay up for yourselves treasures in heaven."

—Matt. 6:19-20

SOME OF THE WORLD'S GREATEST TREASURES HAVE BEEN LEFT TO us by men who died either penniless or with almost no money.

The first and greatest example we remember is our Lord and Savior, Jesus Christ, whose Father and our Father owns the whole universe and all in it, yet had only the clothing he wore when he died. No house, no bank account, no chest of gold hidden away, not even a purse to keep money in. Because he left no money for his mother, Mary, he asked his beloved disciple John to take care of her. But how rich was the world because of Jesus' life!

Just a few years ago Frederick M. Vinson, Chief Justice of the United States Supreme Court, the highest judge in the land, died after thirty years of faithful service to his country in many public offices. None of them paid very much, but he cared more for service to his fellow man than for riches. When he died, he left behind only a few thousand dollars, less than ten thousand, to be exact! But our land is better and finer for Frederick M. Vinson's faithful and devoted service.

Thomas Jefferson, author of the Declaration of Independence, President of the United States, and one of its greatest patriots, built a lovely home, Monticello, just outside the town of Charlottesville, Virginia. He loved this brick mansion, which still stands as he built it. But because he received so little pay for his public work and his expenses were so high, he was forced to mortgage Monticello. This meant he borrowed money and said he would give the lender his home if he couldn't pay it back. Jefferson died without any money—this great patriot and one of America's greatest men. He put his country first and himself last.

Wolfgang Mozart was one of the world's greatest musicians. The music he wrote nearly two hundred years ago in his native Austria is loved and played everywhere. God gave to him a remarkable power to compose beautiful melodies. Although he died while only thirty-five, he left many, many great works of music.

But did he make money? No. He was poorly paid. Also, he was a poor manager in money affairs. When he died in 1791, only the cheapest kind of funeral was held. No friends went to the cemetery to see him buried. Soon the exact location of his grave was forgotten, and today nobody knows really where this great man's body was laid. To make matters worse, he was buried in the pauper's cemetery, that is, in the cemetery set aside by the city for poor people whose families couldn't buy any ground anywhere else. How rich the world is, though, because of Mozart's music!

Many other great men have died poor after having made our world a better place to live.

Surely God does not want us to neglect those we love. Certainly he wants us to provide our families with enough food, clothing, and other necessary things.

But we can easily believe, as so many do, that making money and buying things are what God wants us to do most of all. Many people pile up riches and leave the world poorer. They become greedy, selfish, and spoiled. Jesus warned us against the love of money and said it could destroy our souls.

Are you making the world richer or poorer? Even if you have no money, you can make it a better place than you found it.

41. Making Your Weak Points Your Strong Points

"Do your best to present yourself to God as one approved, a workman who has no need to be ashamed."
—II Tim. 2:15

GLENN CUNNINGHAM OF KANSAS AT ONE TIME HELD THE WORLD'S speed record for running the mile. He was called the "Iron Man" so great was his endurance. Yet not many years before he won race after race in college track meets, Glenn Cunningham's parents were told he would never even walk. He had been badly burned in a tragic fire, and terrible scars prevented free movement of his legs.

But the boy Glenn determined to run. He went on and on, training twice as hard as other boys without his handicap. Today we remember him as one of America's greatest athletes. Glenn Cunningham made a weak point into a strong point.

Turn back the pages of history to the ancient Greeks. A boy named Demosthenes of Athens had some kind of speech defect. Perhaps he stuttered. Perhaps he couldn't pronounce certain letters or make certain sounds. If you know any boy or girl with a speech defect, you know how terrible it can make them feel. And always there are children rude and unkind enough to poke fun at others born with such troubles.

But did this handicap stop Demosthenes? Not on your life. Instead of staying away from people, he went to a teacher of oratory, that is, one who teaches public speaking, and got instruction. For years he worked and worked. According to one legend, which is probably just a story and nothing more, Demosthenes put pebbles in his mouth and shouted speeches to the sea. Whether true or not it shows that the Greeks gave honor to one who overcame his handicaps, for this same Demosthenes was acclaimed in his day as the greatest orator of them all. So great, in fact, that now, over 2,300 years later, we remember him. His life could have turned out differently. He could have

93

been ashamed of his speech difficulty and not tried to overcome it.

Franklin D. Roosevelt stands out in memory as one who, afflicted with polio with both legs paralyzed, so increased his will power and character through his struggle against being crippled that he became President of the United States. When Roosevelt was stricken in 1921, most of his close friends said, "He's finished in public life!" Desperate years followed. In 1932 this crippled man was elected our President.

But getting well himself was not enough. Franklin D. Roosevelt wanted to prevent others from getting the disease of polio. He started the "March of Dimes," which finally led to the Salk vaccine.

Once I knew a well-to-do lady who was known for her generosity with poor children and for her many acts of assistance to boys and girls with little chance in life. One day she told me the secret of her greatness. She said, "When I was a little girl, I had no parents. I was fourteen years old before anybody ever gave me a party of any kind."

She was trying to give other children a better chance than she herself had ever had as a girl. And how well she succeeded! Nobody has more friends than she. She turned a point of weakness into a point of strength.

Sometimes God sends us trouble in order to strengthen us. Perhaps he means for certain difficulties to be steppingstones to growing up. At least that's the way we can best use them.

We have weak points, all of us. In overcoming them we become stronger and better. Ask God to help you, for he always will.

42. Don't Let God Down

"You are my friends if you do what I command you."
—John 15:14

THE SADDEST MOMENT IN BASEBALL'S LONG HISTORY WAS NOT when the mythical Casey swung out with bases loaded. Nor was it when Babe Ruth or Lou Gehrig or Dizzy Dean or Frankie Frisch or Joe Dimaggio or any of the other immortals of baseball history played their last game.

No, the saddest moment in organized baseball was late in 1919. The place was not a ball park but the sidewalk outside the Cook County courthouse in Chicago when a national baseball hero, member of the American League winning Chicago White Sox for that year (they lost the World Series to Cincinnati), admitted that he had accepted a bribe from a gambler to help lose the series.

Many other players were involved, but this one was the most famous and best loved. As he stepped from inside the courthouse, where he and his teammates had been questioned about the bribes, a small newsboy, one of his idols, stepped up from a group of boys waiting for news and pleaded, "It ain't so, is it, Joe?"

"Yes," he replied. "I guess it is, boys."

Without any evil intent this player let millions of boys down. They thought he could do no wrong. But like all of us, he could and did. Out of the scandals of that World Series came a new setup for professional baseball. Never since has there been any slight hint of crookedness.

We never know how much somebody depends on us for inspiration, help, and guidance. We are never too unimportant to be a good example. And when we do something to let our friends down, it pains them and us deep inside. This is perhaps one of the harshest penalties for wrongdoing—the knowledge that somebody else is hurt.

Connected with the death of Jesus were two men whose

95

hearts broke because they let him down. One was Judas, who for thirty pieces of silver betrayed his Master. When he saw what a terrible thing he had done, he killed himself. His own feelings punished him.

The other man was Peter, who said three times he didn't know Jesus. After the third time he went out and wept bitterly. Unlike Judas he made up for his cowardice later by living boldly for Christ. But how much he suffered inside!

Have you ever had a close friend let you down—take sides against you in school or on the way home, or join other boys or girls in making you miserable? Most of us know what it's like to be betrayed. It hurts inside. Since we know, we should remember that our actions may hurt other people in the same manner.

God, too, depends on us. He is our greatest friend. Though he might seem invisible and faraway, he is always near. When other friends move away, he stays. When others leave us, he remains. And he counts on us to be true to him.

Because God is so great, you might think that what we do doesn't matter much to him. How can he know or care? we might ask. But he does know. He does care. Jesus told us God knows even the number of hairs on our heads.

Best of all is the willingness of God to give us another chance when we do wrong. Certainly he is hurt, but he does forgive. Just as Jesus forgave Peter, so God forgives us.

Don't let your parents and friends down. Keep clean the faith they have in you. And be willing to forgive others when they, too, like all human beings do sometime or other, fail to keep faith with you.